The Next World

Our Expanding Consciousness

For Carolyn —
Being & becoming
better humans
moves evolution

Jennifer Shoals

Copyright © 2023 Jennifer Shoals

All rights reserved. No part of this book my be used or reproduced by any means, graphic, electronic, or mechanical, including photocopying, recording, taping, or by any information storage retrieval system without the written permission of the author except in the case of brief quotations embodied in articles and reviews.

ISBN: 978-1-7341987-0-6 (sc)
ISBN: 978-1-7341987-3-7 (e)

Library of Congress Control Number: 9781734198706

Shoals. Jennifer.
The Next World, Our Expanding Consciousness / Jennifer Shoals.
— Thunder Bird

1. Transcendence 2. Consciousness 3. Personal Growth 4. Channeling I. Title

Books may be ordered through booksellers or by contacting:
Thunder Bird
PO Box 776
Grand Marais, MN 55604
www. jennifershoals.com

The author of this book does not dispense medical advice or prescribe the use of any technique as a form of treatment for physical, emotional, or medical problems without the advice of a physician, either directly or indirectly. The intent of the author is only to offer information of a general nature to help you in your quest for emotional and spiritual well-being. In the event that you use any of the information in this book for yourself, which is your constitutional right, the author and the publisher assume no responsibility for your actions.

Cover art: Sweetwater Design Company, sweetwaterdesignco.com
Cover photo courtesy of: Kristaps Ungurs, unsplash.com/@kristapungurs

Printed in the United States of America
Lightning Source / Ingram Spark

*For Zahir, Melanie, Amy, Nancy, Gene, and Abby
—with great thanks for your support and encouragement*

*With gratitude for all the travelers—past, present and future:
we are the journey
of our spirits walking
the Earth*

Contents

Introduction: Our Expanding Consciousness (ix)

1. Star Travel   1

2. Destination Unknown   37

3. Vibrational Healing   65

4. Empathy, Love and Compassion   97

5. Heavenly Journeys   125

6. Dimensional Evolution   167

7. The Path With Joy   207

Introduction

Our Expanding Consciousness

With ever-expanding communication and the realization of a shared planet, we have become global citizens. At the same time, changes during the pandemic years have drawn us inward, toward our spiritual lives and our communities. As a whole, we are traveling a path toward a broader view of ourselves and the universe. We are participating in a shift in consciousness.

Ancient cultures practiced an expanded consciousness which included energies beyond the confines of Time and the Physical World. What if we, too, could access those energies and connect with the eternal cosmos? Deep history and universal truths would appear, wisdom that could enrich our lives and aide our survival.

For over twenty years I have been practicing this kind of communication. Through a state of alert relaxation I have learned to open myself to worlds beyond the five senses. In this state I receive transmissions from spiritual teachers. The first Teachers to visit were my own grandmothers, long gone and coming to me from the Spirit World. This channel gradually grew to include many of my ancestors, both known and unknown, as well as the wealth of information available through Universal Wisdom (also called the Collective Unconscious).

The Teachers come to me through a variety of voices from different cultures, age groups, genders, and historical times. I do not represent or speak for any of these groups. The Teachers speak and I record their words. Our intention, together, is to foster greater understanding.

Throughout our books, the Teachers are identified by their name in bold, and their words appear in italics. During transmission, I type what I am told—I do not edit their words. In that way, being a channel is somewhat like taking dictation. Because they are not limited by Time, however, the teachings do not arrive in linear order. Not all of the information on one topic comes at once. My job as a writer is to link idea patterns in the messages and create connections between them.

The stories that the Teachers share vary but their message is always one of Love, compassion, spiritual connection, and expanded consciousness. They are encouraging us to move our awareness beyond the five senses, and to use this increased awareness to live in harmony with ourselves and each other and the universe. They are asking us to move, intentionally, to the next level of spiritual evolution.

The collective wealth of these teachings has been brought together in the *Inspiring Deeper Connections* book series. Here the Teachers acknowledge that we are coming through a time of change, a monumental shift in energy, and urge us to become active participants in it. Part of this shift is a movement beyond Ego to include Spirit—away from functioning in the physical plane *only* and toward the inclusion of energy dimensions beyond it.

The first book looks at the limits of five-sense-only living and asks us to create a spirit-fed life.[1] The second book explores how our lives interact with the Universe and encourages us to practice integrating Spirit into the Physical World.[2] In this third book, the Teachers are inspiring us to expand our consciousness, to personally experience multiple dimensions and bring this vibrational aware-

---

[1] *Grandmother Dreams, Conversations Across the Veil*, (self-pub./Thunder Bird, Ingram Spark, 2012).

[2] *Traveling Light, Moving Our Awareness Beyond the Five Senses* (self-pub./Thunder Bird, Ingram Spark, 2019).

ness into our everyday lives.

The words of wisdom shared by the Teachers can be used in several ways. I have used them to navigate personal crises and heal deep trauma. Along the way I became less reactive, more grounded, and more open. Many readers report that these books provide a calming perspective and a deeper connection with the spiritual world, renewing their higher purpose.

We can also use this information to support the current shift in the evolution of human spirituality. Investment in organized religion is waning, as people seek a spiritual lifestyle which is more inclusive and creatively connected. This is the kind of spirituality my Teachers describe. Their messages nurture the sensations of awareness and expansion. They inspire us to see ourselves in the Universe and the Universe in ourselves and others. They connect us through common ground and shared energy dimensions in an expanded consciousness that is available to everyone.

There are many ways to read these books. You can start with the first book and read them in order, or you can read any one book that calls to you. I have found it helpful to read the books out loud, either with another person or in a group. The resulting discussions are very rich. Each book can be read in the traditional way—starting at page one and going to the end. You can also use the 'Book Fairy' technique: open the book at random, wherever feels right, and just connect to the information on that page. Many readers say that they do this regularly and always find something helpful. I do too.

These teachings contain concepts, guidance and support for more balanced living. They are not, however, an intellectual exercise. They are not something to study, memorize and regurgitate. The information originates from beyond the five senses and the messages hold this extra-dimensional energy within them. The goal is to create an inner experience which harmonizes our vibration with the Universe. As you read, acknowledge your feelings and welcome the energy transfer that accompanies the wisdom. Follow through by bringing the source and the echoes of these vibrations into your daily life.

In all of their conversations, the Teachers appear to be sharing information with *me*. As you read along, however, always understand that the word "you" does not apply only to me, the receiver and recorder of these conversations. It also applies to *you*, the reader. Always insert yourself into the discussion. I am the channel, and the Teachers are speaking to everyone.

> *"I am a little pencil
> in the hand of a writing God
> who is sending a love letter
> to the world."*
>
> ~ Mother Teresa

I have been asked many times about the use of the word 'God' in my books. It is such a small word, only three letters, yet it is loaded with heavy baggage. There are so many alternatives—why don't I use something else?

The word 'God' does, of course, have many meanings. *All* words are symbols. They borrow history from linguistics and then create emotional attachment with their ongoing use. As a child, we might have been taught that God is a bearded white guy sitting up in the clouds, separate from us. This entity is variously seen as an all-knowing observer, uplifting protector, puppeteer, and punisher. Because of these representations, I have been hesitant to promote the use of the word.

My Teachers, however, prefer the word 'God' and have asked me to use it. Free of religious context, it is a term that immediately connects our psyche to a deep spiritual reference. The Teachers use the word in a very broad sense, to describe an expansive energy:

A'riquea:[3] *As you know, God is not an entity or a personality—those are human constructs. God is energy. It is the energy of One Love, the movement of Life Force, the white light of Pure Radiance. It is beyond your capacity to comprehend in human form. Only when you are outside of human form can you truly join God.*

That does not mean that you cannot experience God while you are in human form. You can, and you must. That is your Purpose—to find God's Pure Love on Earth. To use your physical form to move God energy. Through yourself and others. These are the connecting points—to become capable of embodying this Love energy and moving it towards others. This energy movement is what is needed in the Universe.

When spiritual travel occurs, the energy that we travel with is God. The "place" that we travel is the Universe. It is all interwoven.

Universal Wisdom:[4] *God is a force, a form of energy. God is all of the energies of living combined. Not just humans, but all living combined. And not just the present, but all lifetimes and layers combined. God is very powerful in this way. God is all of the knowing and also all of the unknowing, all of the action and all of the action not taken. It is why what you choose to think and feel and do is so important—it all adds into the whole which is God. It is constantly being formed…*

The Universe is Everything. It is the living and the non-living and more than that as well. There is so much that humans will never see, because you are blinded by the dream of physical reality that you function in. This is not a problem, it is a gift, because there is so much richness to the experiences you share with God when you are in physical form. It can be a problem when you forget that there is existence beyond the physical dream.

The purpose of this work is to help people come back to the

---

[3] **A'riquea** (Ah-REE-kee-ah) is a young Black woman with rosy cheeks. Her voice is soft and gentle. She often teaches me about the connecting points of spiritual energy and interpersonal intimacy.

[4] **Universal Wisdom** is the aggregate of all the wisdom in the Universe. I do not see or hear it, and it has no personality. It comes to me as energy in words. Another term for this is the Collective Unconscious.

awareness of a world expanded beyond the physical dream—not to discard the physical world, but to include it and move farther into other realms, across the veil. To develop the ability to cross the veil and come back, to share the wisdom gained and integrate it into the physical world—to impact the physical world with the wisdom gained from spiritual travel.

I hope that you enjoy these books and practice the wisdom they contain. It is important to not only find our spiritual path, but to wear it smooth with use.

~ 1 ~

Star Travel

Ancient cultures communicated with plants and animals, water, sky, stars, stone—with everything in the spiritual flow of life. They recognized shared energy space with all, including those who had gone before. These connections helped ensure the integrity of their environment and were absolutely necessary for survival.

All humans alive today, every one of us, are the offspring of these ancient cultures. Technology and our modern world may have limited our connections with spiritual intuition, but it is still there. Dormant. Ready. In order to re-unite with the timeless Universe, we need only return to something that our cells already know. When we let go of the intellect and its the need to analyze and label, we free ourselves to make this journey.

> "We are the Earth people on a spiritual journey to the stars.
> Our quest, our Earth walk, is to look within,
> to know who we are, to see that we are connected
> to all things, that there is no separation,
> only in the mind."
>
> ~ Lakota

Many years ago I made a pilgrimage to Pine Ridge in South Dakota. I did not know why—the spirits called and I went. I was drawn to the cemetery at the site of Wounded Knee, where in 1890 hundreds of unarmed Lakota families were gunned down by the U.S. military.

I knelt on the ground there, in a pouring rain, unable to stop weeping at the tragedy. Making an offering, my light-skinned outer body asked forgiveness from the brown-skinned who had been murdered there. In the moment of asking, my light skin peeled back to reveal Brown Being, a brown layer underneath, connecting me to All Our Ancestors. This brown-skinned self granted compassionate forgiveness for the unforgivable. In the moment of forgiveness, the brown layer peeled back to reveal the entire Universe inside me, The One With All. I became the infinite night sky full of stars, and was given the name Star Sky Forever.

Everyone has access to this infinity of stars, because we are all made of them. Our purpose on Earth is to travel there and bring back the wisdom of that travel. The following teaching explains this.

Before I pray, I clear the energy by smudging myself and my area with sage. It helps me to feel lighter, more clear. I marvel at the smoke curling around the room, through the air, across the sunbeams. A Native Teacher[5] came to me in a dream and showed me how this smoke works.

The smoke in the dream was similar to that of the sage, but thicker. The smoke rose up into the black empty space around us, lit from below in some way, highlighting it. It curled into a rotating column, forming a kind of wispy smoke tube reaching heavenward. The Teacher showed me this smoke and this effect, and wordlessly

---

[5] There are several terms used to identify the vast cultures of The People who were already in North America when Europeans arrived. Politically correct labels vary over time and geography. In previous books I used the term "Indian" because the Indigenous people that I know prefer that term. Times have changed over the decades since then, and I now use the words Native or Indigenous.

explained that this is prayer. Smoke prayer. Beautiful.

In the dream he then invited me to return to the work that has been asked of me. I want to be open to this. I say: I am practicing opening. I am in service to the spirits that were here, on this land, before I came, before the Europeans came. I am in service to the energy which is now rising, in many places, to bring unity to the people and harmony to the planet. I wish to nourish this change, whatever that means. I apologize—I cannot speak your language. My intention is for greater understanding.

The Teacher smiles and looks down quietly. He speaks to me with his mind.

Robert:[6] *This I will tell you. We are part of the All That Is, this Great Mystery which is unexplainable. There are the stars* [he points to the night sky]. *See how many there are. So many. It is breath-taking to feel this in your body. That is because feeling this connects the stars in the sky with all of the stars in your body, in the body of every living thing, which is every thing. Every thing is living, has a relationship to something else. We are all related. And the We is everything.*

When you connect the stars in the sky with the stars in your body, then you are connecting with the energy that is all of the space that all of the stars exist in. There is the Great Mystery—in the space where everything exists.

You are a beautiful child. You are a child of the Universe, and you have chosen to be born into this physical life, bringing all of the stars along with you in your physical body. You bring them along so that you continue the connection.

Your journey on this Earth is simply to live with the stars, to make sure that the constellations within your body are honored and loved, to shine them up with love and beauty. To know that the constellations in your body, the stars in your body, are pieces of the constellations in the

---

[6]**Robert** is a Native man with longish hair, hanging free with some beading in the front strands. He wears a mix of Western and Native clothing, several layers. He has a benevolent face, lined with wisdom wrinkles of knowledge. His eyes express both deep sadness and great joy in living.

sky. It is all connected.

You may feel that you are far away from those stars in the sky, but you are no more distant than those stars are to other stars in the sky. The distances are vast when you look from this view. But when you see the whole context, you see that everything is within reach.

Dance with the ancestors, whose stars have made yours and whose stars are, like yours, connected to all of the other stars. When you dance with the ancestors, you are dancing a future for your grandchildren, and your great-grandchildren. You are dancing the Universe into being.

Say your prayers with this in *mind. Say your prayers with* this mind. *Bring your future into the present, in a circle, in a swirling gateway of smoke, a tunnel you will travel when it is your turn to join the ancestors, a tunnel you may travel in this world, when the stars are aligned. It is up to you. To make this journey, over and over and over. To create a path that others may travel, when they are ready. You do not make their journey for them, you only make the path.*

Go now, with your good intentions, and manifest them on the physical plane, in the sky of stars, in the space that connects them. Make your path with prayer.

Our journey to the stars, the walk inward that takes us outward, occurs in a realm outside of Time. Everyone who has ever been born and everyone who is yet to be born travels in this realm. In this way, we are all immigrants, in constant motion. Joining the energy of this movement is what is sometimes referred to as Star Travel. This is how it was explained to me:

Helmut:[7] *I am the son of an immigrant. I am going to tell you the traveling songs.*

The people of the Earth are in constant motion, over long periods of time, like water flowing over the Earth. There is movement,

---

[7]**Helmut** is a short, stout man of great physical strength, born in Eastern Europe in the mid-1800s.

joining, parting, pooling. You think you can trace your heritage back to a known source. This is false. There is only one source, lost to Time, but known to Life. It is when Life Force chose a new path, and made the being who walks on two legs, a being who walks all over the Earth, not just in one place.

We can tell you that story, but it is not the traveling song. It is only where the traveling songs came from. Because we are always traveling.

We came from a place without Time, and we entered into one of Time. When we entered Time, that is when we began traveling, for then there was a starting point, a place to come from and another place to go to, with movement in between. That movement is the journey that we are all traveling on. We are on that journey. We are walking. We are moving.

That is the changing, the shifting, the sea of energy in motion. It is where we will enter the New World, in that sea of movement, on that journey. There is no stopping, only the illusion of fixing Time into a moment. Energy is moving, always moving, between Points. It is walking. It is traveling. Being two-legged means walking, means traveling, not just on the Earth but through the journey of Space.

When you travel in Space, star energy is collecting on your clothing, like burrs in a field, as you travel the fields of Space. You are bathing in the healing pool of star energy, of all the dimensions that belong in the Universe. It is the reason to do this, to travel in Space. You are traveling in the place you came from, where you go back to, and bringing with you the gifts of your walking. You are moving energy: you are energy that is moving, and you are collecting energy and moving it. This is the beginning of your Next World.

Helmut's directive is to travel and to bring back the gifts of our walking. The travel he is referring to is a spiritual pilgrimage, but it is similar in effect to going on a trip to a new country. Travel to far away places exposes us to new ways of thinking and being, it stretches our psyche. Once we return home, we will never be exactly the same as we were before we left. We will have changed. This is the reason to travel.

It is important for individuals to expand their horizons in this way. When many people are doing this then we will see changes on an evolutionary scale. This is what is being asked of us—to practice Star Travel because it both improves us and also enriches the whole.

The Library Man:[8] *This is something that needs to be understood, even though it cannot be understood. Once you have done it, you will have the memory of having done it imbedded in your energy. If you have not done it, you will not be able to understand it.*

This is a time of much learning, with many people seeking this learning. The more people travel, the easier it will be to travel, because the channels will be more open, the flow of these channels will help to bring more people into them.

It is also a difficult time of learning, because some people have to make the leap, and it is harder to do when the channels do not have much energy in them. Yet. So it will be up to you to find these people, these channels. You are going to have to go some places that are not that comfortable, where you may not feel welcome, but where you know the forces are at work. You will open your eyes and begin seeing energy moving, and you will need to follow those trails to their source. As you know, things are not always as they seem.

I heard today that "seeing is not believing, believing is seeing."

It is not just believing. It is seeing. Seeing energy in motion. A new level of awareness will develop, and you must follow that awareness. You have been telling people that following their intuition will help to develop channeling. This is true for you, too, but on a different level. You must develop another sense, a sense that is aware of energy moving, and then follow the energy to its source. Follow the energy to its source. I cannot

---

[8]**The Library Man** is a scholar who comes to me to talk about metaphysics. I often meet him in a classroom with a large chalkboard or an office stacked with papers. He is a scientist in a white lab coat, with wild white hair and a thick West-Germanic accent.

say that enough. Not just follow the energy, but follow it to its source. Return to the original seed, the seed of knowing.
You can say this, and it would be true. But the thing that has to happen is to do it. Not just think about it, but do *it.*

Spiritual travel, the next layer of consciousness, is not just something to think or talk about. Having a direct experience is something that touches all aspects of our being—our mind, our body, our emotions, our spirit—on cellular and subatomic levels. Doing it creates a deep understanding of our connection to The Everything.

෴

What is this Star Travel? At the beginning of my own channeling journey, I prepared by practicing physical energy movement and quiet meditation. I learned to be both fully in my mind-body and simultaneously expanded beyond it. This is the state of alert relaxation also known as transcendence.

In this state I travel beyond the veil, the thin division in awareness between five-sense reality and other realities beyond it. There, I receive deep teachings. Over time, I realized that there are many ways that Star Travel manifests. All of them occur in this deep state of alert relaxation.

Sometimes, I am shown dimensions where others are traveling. I had many of these experiences during the year of my father's dying. Some very specific ones occurred right at his death. They all highlight the vast worlds that exist within our range.

After my dad had taken his final breaths, I sat with him. I pulled a chair to his bedside and leaned over, resting my face and shoulders next to his. While I was lying there with him, I looked up to the place near the ceiling where I had previously seen the white path leading to the Spirit World. Over the course of several months, my father's spirit had tried to swim up that path, but he never reached the top before coming back down to the bed. I had seen my mother there too, waiting to receive him. When I asked her why she didn't take him, she said that he wasn't ready.

On the day my father passed, both my mother and the Spirit World were visible. My mother had made a beautiful white bed in a white room for her husband. Brilliant white. She was waiting for him to enter and rest. The Spirit World appeared as a brilliant white cloud of lovely energy, gently billowing downward into the room. All of it was peaceful and welcoming.

At my father's funeral, I spent some time alone with him at the casket before the viewing started. I checked in to see if I could connect with him. I relaxed into a meditative state and he came right away. He was absolutely gleeful. He was so full of joy that he was ready to burst. Anyone who had ever seen him like that in life would recognize it in an instant—his eyes wide, his body taut with excitement, his grin so broad that his cheeks almost disappeared.

He said excitedly, "I want to show you something!" I followed him. He was moving along up in the clouds. We could see the Earth far below, green fields and forests. We stayed at cloud level and he brought me to a huge white palace. The palace had a red door in it. With great excitement and expectation, he said, "Look at this!" He opened the door to reveal a lively social scene, with lots of people laughing and eating, glasses and silverware clinking—something he really enjoyed doing. He closed the red door. Then he said, "Now look at *this*!" and he opened the exact same door again. The inside had instantly transformed into a giant library, with wooden reading tables and chairs, walls lined with books stretching 20 feet to the ceiling—another thing he really loved. Still gleeful, he closed the door, and was about to open it again when another family member walked up to his casket in the church. Allowing for their privacy, I got up and left. I don't know what else my father was going to show me. He was clearly thrilled with both of those situations.

I think his point was that heaven is whatever you want it to be. When I tried to check in with him again later I saw him far in the distance, running joyfully away into the clouds. He had his arms wide open in elation, ready to take in everything that heaven had to offer.

I thought about those situations, those views of heaven, later while I was out on a walk. I was walking on a snowy road and it occurred to me that I could actually be walking in heaven right then. I thought about heaven and hell as states of being manifested right here on earth.

Walking in 'heaven' would mean being fully present, spiritually, and not attached to ego. 'Hell' would be the opposite, being fully attached to ego and *not* spiritually present. But then I thought about the horrible situations that humans can be placed in such as sex trafficking, slave labor, concentration camps. That is hell on earth. I suppose it could be argued that we are capable of finding heaven wherever we are, and those are just the most extreme circumstances. I have often been drawn to stories of the Holocaust and the Gulags, because there were always people there who somehow managed to practice Love, compassion and forgiveness even in those terrible situations. But the heaven that my father showed me was the most wonderful place, designed specifically to his preferences. Maybe this dimension of heaven is made to reconnect the spirit with Joy and fully positive energy?

This is fascinating to me. Of course, there is more to the physical world than most humans perceive. But what are all of these other "places"? What is the Dream World? What is Heaven?

Someone strides out into my view—a large strong woman in flowing African fibers, with dark skin and great physical presence. She has her hair wound in a scarf. She seats herself on a large chair, like a throne, with both her feet squarely planted on the floor, her arms resting on the flat wooden arms of the chair. Her voice is deep and resonant. She has the accent of someone whose first language is tribal.

A'dziimbuuma:[9] *You would like all of these things to fit together in*

---

[9] (Ahd-zee-EEM-boo-oom-ah)

a way is that is easy to explain. The world is not put together in such a way. There are always things that do not fit into the story, and that is just the way it is. That is just the way it is.

You cannot explain how you yourself fit into this story. Because the story is much larger than any you can ever know. The story is not one told by humans, with the rest of the world in it. The story is being told by the Universe, and humans happen to be in it.

You will travel well when you can take yourself away from the human-told story. Then you will be able to see small bits of the rest of the story. You will never see all of that story while you are in human form. Just small bits.

But you can travel to other parts of the story. The reason to take such a journey is not so that you can come back and report on this or that and fit it into the human story. The journey itself is what changes you. Like going to a foreign land. You can never fully grasp what that world is, because you do not come from there, you were not born into it. The best you can do is travel, and bring back with you the change that has occurred in yourself, apply it to the place you return. This is the Shift you are being asked to create. It is a change in your energy state that you will apply to the human story. The vibrations will be changed, and so the story will be changed. That is how evolution occurs.

I am thinking of climate change, and how we are destroying many life forms by our actions. (I have a vision of a beautiful giraffe, and what an amazing creation this is, how sad it will be if she is erased.) *This is the human story interacting with the Earth's story. It is but one of the areas that needs to change. There are many, and they are all related, in communication with each other. In communication through energy vibration. This is what needs to change, and you can effect this by taking the journey. Not going to a place, but by journeying there.*

We are going to be teaching you through this medium. You must prepare yourself, prepare your body, prepare your relationships. You must be aligned. And then you will go.

With great thanks, my Mother, I hear your words. With great gratitude, I journey forth.

She slaps both hands on the arms of her chair, stomps both feet on the floor. We are done.

Witnessing others as they navigate the Spirit World is one way to travel. Dreaming while asleep is another. The more practiced I am in waking conversation with spiritual teachers, for example, the more active I am in my dreams. I am not just an observer, I am *in* them. I have agency—I interact with other people, make choices, and take action based on those choices. I step through and in and out of other dimensions. My sleeping dreams are another functional dimension. There are so many layers!

I had a dream once where I saw a group of Native men meeting with my father. They were having a deep discussion, making decisions. I approached the leader, a man named Earl, and was told this was not my business. My father sent me away. When I awoke, I was told:

Universal Wisdom: *You would like to be able to pinpoint a meaning to this dream, a meaning that would tell you how to conduct your life, what to expect. It is not so simple. There are undercurrents occurring many places where you cannot see them. In this dream, you had a glimpse into something that did not directly concern you. That is why your father sent you away. People in dreams take shapes that you relate to, but that is not necessarily who they are. You were right to respect your elder and stay away. Earl is someone who may materialize, but not in a way that you recognize.*

Like my teacher Eagle Brother,[10] who seems to have a dual life that even he is not aware of.

Yes. Everyone is working on multiple planes. It's like tuning to a radio channel. They are all there, it just depends where you set the dial, where

---

[10] **Eagle Brother** (also called **Migizi Niikaan**) is an actual person in the physical world, although he has a life very separate from mine and I hardly know him. In the Dream World, I am married to him—he is my Spirit Husband. This is discussed in detail in *Traveling Light*, p. 185-98.

you rest your attention. You are often resting in the fuzzy static between channels in your current life. Sometimes you seem to be distressed by this. It takes a lot of energy to keep tuning in and out. Even the physical world takes a certain amount of energy to maintain. Resting in the static is what your current state can integrate. You have been over-sensitized by the flood of chemotherapy toxin to your body. You cannot decide to just ignore that and move along. Recovering is a very slow process, and you won't ever be the way you before the poisoning.

I know it is already done, I can't go back and undo it. But I wonder if I made a bad choice to take chemo.

There is a bigger picture to this that you are not seeing. Placed in the context of decades, this is just a part of your life spent in the shadows. Like taking a nap during the day. You are a little checked out, but that is what you need to do to be ready for the next part.

Interesting to think of my entire life as just one day. Born early in the morning, working hard as an adult at high noon. I'm taking a late afternoon nap now. Resting up for the evening of my elder years. That makes me smile.

Keep that in mind.

In addition to observing activity in the Spirit World and inter-acting in my sleeping dreams, beings sometimes come from other worlds to open my awareness in five-sense physical reality. The following example occurred after I awoke from a sleeping dream:

In my sleep I dreamed that I was outdoors, and a dog brought me a bird in its mouth. The bird was a sleek electric blue and black, with wings neatly folded and unhurt in the dog's soft mouth. I smoothed out the feathers and released the bird into the sky, where it flew away. Afterward I wondered if I'd done the right thing in releasing it.

Then the dog brought another bird and I also released it. As I looked up into the sky, the bird opened its wings and hung in the air fully extended. It was black and red, the exact color and shape of the thunderbird on my chest.[11] I was alarmed to think that I had released this bird into the winter sky and it would not be able to survive the cold. I called for it to come back. It was a wild bird, and not likely to do so. I was lying on my back on the ground, with my arms out-stretched into the air, begging it to come back. It flew a short distance and then turned, coming back to hover over me. It was suspended high in the air, looking down at me, its talons reaching out, when I woke up.

After I awoke, I didn't know what to make of this dream. How could I possibly be responsible for a wild bird? I think there is something here about letting the bird, the power of the bird, be out in the larger world. I do not own or control this power, I only borrow it, or it borrows me. In my waking life at the time, I had been regularly concentrating on the energy of "nurturing my bird," my animal power, the Thunderbird. This is the energy I want to embody, to bring out into the world and encourage—spiritual presence.

As I opened my consciousness to multi-dimensional discussion, I became filled with a strong and intense power at the realization of a Teacher's presence, a Thunder Being:

Aniimaakii:[12] *The Thunder Beings work in their own ways. You are a small piece of a much larger picture. Sometimes you will not have the vantage point of this larger picture and you will not understand what is occurring.*

It was right to release the bird. You cannot keep this bird to yourself. It is active in other realms and other dreams. You are helping it to do this work when you release it. This happens on a regular basis during your sleep time. You are not usually aware of it happening. It is good for you to know that this is happening, that the Thunder Being is operating on a bigger scale, and that it is going to be renewed as you

---

[11] I have a full-chest tattoo whose presence is two-fold: reclaiming my body after the disfigurement of cancer surgery, and embodying the spiritual purpose of my living.

[12] (Ah-nee-mah-kee)

sleep.

> *If you want the Thunder Being to take you on its journey, you will have to be willing to shift your energy shape. This is not as difficult as it sounds, but you do not have this skill yet. You will need to learn how to do this. It means that you learn how to change the configuration of your energy, into something that lines up with the place you are going. You will want to do this.*

Miigwech [Thank you]. I feel my purpose renewed with this conversation.

It will be important to look at how you prioritize your time, for that is the same as prioritizing your energy. Make activities that feed your spirit be the first things you do. Getting caught up in busy-ness means there is little energy left for the important work of spiritual development and spiritual learning. I am the next Teacher, and you must make time for me. We have work to do.

Yes, of course. This is my purpose, and I feel stronger when I am aligned with it.

[He knows my thoughts, he knows that I am struggling to find the words, when what I really need is to make an energy commitment. Clearly, I need to look at my priorities and get straight.]

I've had many energy experiences related to this Thunderbird on my chest. It is part of me, an embodied spiritual energy. It makes its presence known even when I am not thinking about it.

I was in a meeting once, and there was a thunderbird painted on the wall. When I casually looked at it, the energy on my chest leapt out to meet the thunderbird on the wall. I had a powerful physical sensation, like an electrical shock, and a connection was made.

Another time, in a waking vision, a handful of Native men arrived at my door. They were casually dressed, just hanging out. They were checking out the stuff in my yard and not looking directly at me, but definitely aware of me standing in the doorway. I was wondering if I should welcome them inside and offer them food, when the Thunderbird on my chest suddenly became energized and all of the men were simultaneously drawn into it. Their images became fluid and they swirled into the Thunderbird as if it were a vortex. In that instant, I became aware that these 'men' were spirits.

∽

The above examples illustrate interactions between the Physical World and the Dream World, between five-sense reality and larger spiritual dimensions. Many of my journeys take me well beyond the physical world, deeper into other realms. If I go far enough inward, I will come out in the All That Is. Then I expand beyond physical boundaries and cross the veil. This is the place that Helmut was talking about moving—among the stars.

I can adjust my energy and place my attention in the space between stars, the healing pool of star energy. It is expansive. It is the dark night sky, illuminated by starlight. When I wonder what the stars are, I can feel myself getting pulled toward one. It is a very bright light, with brilliant spokes of light streaming out from it. I see my hands stretching out ahead of me as I reach toward the star. The spokes of light are bright white but there are also some dark areas, as if shade is being created by something on the surface of the star, or wherever the light is coming from. The "star" is a white ball of energy with giant geometric towers of darkness rising out of it.

I am flying closer and closer, past the towers and toward the surface. The surface is like a swirling white sea of mist, with wisps of white drifting up like the smoke of prayers. Now I am in the white swirling sea. It is like being in a cloud. It is cool and moist and quiet. I can just float in here, quite comfortably, curled up like a fetus.

A Teacher, **Healing Grandmother**, is there standing beside an open frame, a window frame. Beyond it is the Sea of Unknowing. She nods her head once and points to the window. I am to go through it. I reach out and put my hands on the sill. I am weightless and need to steady myself. Then I give the slightest push and I am through.

On the other side, I am once again in the white mist but it seems more like a wall. I can see just over the top of this white wall and below is a green woodland full of plants and animals. I have seen this lush place several times before. Once during a healing, I went to several different planets and one of them was green like this, and all of the animals lived there in harmony with each other. Another time, I almost went through the tunnel of white light during cancer, to the lush green garden at the end, but was pulled back at the last second and the door slammed shut—it was not my time to go.

So it is an Eden of sorts. I hear birds singing and leaves rustling. A lion with a thick mane is laying in the grass. He wishes to speak to me: *You are visiting the world as it once was, the planet of plenty and fertility. You will have to find this place again when your body brings you back. Open to what is not visible in your spectrum. Open to seeing with another sense. Develop this seeing.* The lion has been speaking with a human-like mouth. His body is deflating and changing shape as he talks. It is hard for me to maintain concentration on what is happening. My mind is trying to decide what is "real" and what I am pushing in my own agenda. *Go into the rainbow*, he says as he begins to disappear. *Go into the light of the rainbow. Be the light that creates the rainbow.* His body is like a balloon with the air escaping. He is shriveling and moving away. *Go now.*

Go to the rainbow now, or go away now? *Go away now.* I can no longer see him but I can hear his voice. *Love yourself. Be in the range of all energy.* I feel myself slipping back over the white wall of mist. I am getting pulled back through the window frame. Healing Grandmother waves as I leave the window. I am getting pulled backwards, through the mist, through the dark towers, away from the star, out into black space. I am back in my body.

Traveling in this way is physically refreshing, emotionally freeing, and spiritually inspiring. Many people marvel at this travel and want to know the secrets for accomplishing it themselves. There are no secrets. It requires the practice of alert relaxation and the ongoing experience of an expanded energy state. It is not something to be accomplished or achieved—it is not a project. It is a path. It is a way of being.

A'dziimbuuma: *The thing to keep in mind, the thing to keep in front of your vision, is why you are doing this work. It is not just the work itself. It is the motivation to do the work.*
I believe in it. I see how it has helped me to change in positive ways, to become less reactive and more grounded. It is a place I can come to with vulnerability and in Trust, for help and support. It is a channel for personal and spiritual growth.

I believe that this is what many people are looking for right now, at this time in history. Faith in organized religion is waning, in part because people want a more personal relationship with the Universe. This relationship is much needed, as the planet becomes over-populated and we are crowded closer and closer together. Communication opportunities are now instantaneous. We are being exposed to more and different people, and we need to learn how to accommodate all these differences before we kill each other off. We need to see our place in the Universe so that we honor Nature and our mother ship—Earth. When it all goes to hell, when the climate no longer supports us, money will mean nothing. It will be skills that prevent the extinction of humans. One of those skills is the ability to get along and help each other.

Whoa. I have gone pretty far out.

Not really. When The Shift completes itself, those who leave the planet with energy skills will find them useful in the next dimensions. This is not something that the average person will comprehend. It is one of the reasons to make the changes that we are requesting. There are benefits of many kinds. Some are short term and personal. Some are longer term and social. Others are very long-term and inter-dimensional. You choose where on the continuum you place your attention.

She nods her head twice, slaps her palms twice on the arms of the chair, stamps her feet twice on the floor, then gets up to leave. We are done.

A'dziimbuuma just referred to The Shift. My Teachers have been talking about The Shift for decades. The Shift is a monumental change that is occurring in multiple dimensions simultaneously. It's a kind of cosmic balancing. We do not get to choose whether we participate or not, we only get to choose how. We are being asked to open to these other dimensions which will then further human evolution.

Vast change is not easy, but it is an opportunity to clean house and go forward into a richer life.

As a parallel example, cancer diagnosis and treatment created an enormous upheaval in my personal life. Much of it appeared, initially, to be negative. Unable to function at my job, I lost my income and then could no longer afford to live in my own home. I moved to my studio, a tiny rustic cabin with no running water out in the woods. These were survival circumstances. But the remaking of my life turned out to be a kind of Home-coming which I only saw after I'd made the change. Then I realized its many benefits: Surrounded by bigs trees rooted in the planet and reaching 40 feet into the sky, into the stars, something feels old there—ancient. I named my writing studio Home of the Ancestors, as a way of honoring the spirits and welcoming their energy. I'm connected with Nature hour by hour. I marvel at the beauty. Free of human distraction I feel the enormity of space. Even though I still like to go to town to socialize, human cacophony is gone from my daily life.

One day a thunderstorm was brewing. I have always been excited by that power and I went out in the driveway to greet it. I found myself opening my arms. The Thunderbird on my chest quickened. Its energy met the power of the thunderstorm and there was a vibration between them, a recognition and a celebration. I was communing with the spirits.

I find myself talking out loud in my home in the woods, and not just to myself. I talk to the squirrels and chipmunks, to all the birds, to the plants. The sprouted leaves and flowers are a green fuse inside my own body. They are all my relatives. When I walk, I am aware that I am walking on the Earth. I'm touching the ground beneath my feet, and I'm touching the whole planet. The sky is not just above me, it encircles this planet. Every night when I see the net of starlight through the arms of the trees, I am aware that the stars are also under my feet, around the other side of the world.

This is all very good. Happiness is not the word I would use to describe it. Satisfaction. Harmony. I feel a symbiotic relationship with the Source. Partnering with this energy to make my journey in writing, I am following a directive to help shape the world.

I still have Earthly questions, of course, especially about the manifestation of my books and how to go about that. It is similar to the journey of Star Travel. The process follows similar guidelines: allow the energy to settle and expand, recognize opportunities when they are presented, and follow them. Is there something else I am missing?

Universal Wisdom: *As you know, this cannot be forced. It cannot be willed into existence.*

There is a time for everything. It may not be the timeline you imagine. Remember how everything so far has happened. There is a gradual blending of the spiritual and the physical realms. You seem to be waiting for a dramatic event when that is not how this works. You keep following the path. You keep clearing your energy, cleaning the house of your life. Then one day you will notice that you are in a new place, the place you have been heading all along.

Which is what I have been talking about, landing in my new Home. I have a buzzy feeling in my body.

Talk about it.

It is transcendence. The simultaneous settling and expansion of energy. All of the cells in my body are humming up, vibrating in a way that creates more space between them. The space between cells is connected to all the space around my body, around this building, out in the summer woods, into the blue of the sky, the expanse of Space, the Universe. I am no longer a separate Being. My body is still here, but my energy *is* the Universe. I feel free. Easy. Joyful. At peace. My hands are tingling.

This is where you belong, in the embrace of the Universe. This is the source of pure Action. All choices must align with the Zone. Then you will be on a journey with the stars, the stars will be your companions, and you will become that which your Destiny has created. This is your Soul Path, the place of belonging and harmony with your Creator.

I am on the conveyor belt of my Soul Path, on the way to the Everything. I can see it in the distance. It is a brilliant white light, shooting out powerful rays, like the sun, but white, and the conveyor belt travels right into its center. As I travel closer and closer to the Everything, I am standing with my arms raised and my hands outstretched. I am so close now that there is no more of the Universe visible, except out at the very edges of my sight.

I am entering the white light. My feet are planted and I am being bent backwards with the force of it. It is bathing the arch of my body in the beautiful white light, light so dense that my body is being absorbed into it. I am a little hesitant to let myself be swallowed, in case I cannot come back. But there, I am passing the edge, and I am inside of the white.

It is like a heavy mist, with particles drifting and billowing around me. The particles are tiny black orbs, floating in the warm wet mist. I allow the orbs to pass through my body with the mist. It is all joining the space between my cells. Where the orbs pass through my body, they exit as little fireballs.

And now my body is disassembling, with chunks of it drifting with the waves of mist. I am like a Picasso painting, in 3D. I am being dis-organized. There is an oblong black structure in my head, along the left side of my corpus callosum, the network of nerve fibers that connects both sides of the brain, where my brain injury occurred. It is trying to lift out. It is still attached at the front, like a scab that is not ready to come off. There are some lightning bolts of red and orange and white energy at the connecting point. I have a headache there. I feel pressure on my left eye.

It has been decided to leave it there for now. Before being set back into place, the oblong structure is swirled with the white mist. It is back in place and there is a heaviness, like a rock has been left there. Streams of rainbows are coming out of the top of it and curling around the back and underneath it, joining multi-color lightning bolts at the front. The rainbows split off from there, at my forehead, and unfurl backwards around the outside of my skull, one on each side of my head. They join in the back, at the base of my skull, and then drape down my neck.

The rainbow drape grows, flowing down my back and sides like a cape. A cape of rainbows. It reaches the floor and pools around my feet. Beautiful flowers grow out of the rainbow pool and form a carpet in all directions. The flowers release their scent, like a mist, and it floats upward, into the sky, where it forms clouds. The clouds release a gentle rain that waters the flowers and the rainbows coming out of my head and down my back. The raindrops wash away the rainbows until I am just standing with a hat. The crown of the hat is made of black fiber on the top, with a rainbow band around it, joining at the back with short ends hanging down the nape of my neck. I am wearing a robe of the same rough black fiber, like wool, with rainbow trim at the cuffs, and flowered edging down the front along the zipper. A needlepoint of a large white flower is sewn on the back. I have rainbow slippers.

I raise my hands. My left hand holds a staff. There is a heavy golden metal ball in my right hand. It has some kind of metal decoration on top. There is a line around its horizontal diameter as if it opens and something is held inside. When it hinges open I see a pool in its center. It is a seer's aid. I can jump through its surface and enter the pool. I can put my face through its surface and look into other times. An older white man with a pointed white beard looks up at me. (I have to admit to being a little disappointed that it was not a woman.)

He straightens up, saying *well, we shall see what you are made of, then.*

He points out over a large body of water, showing me a speck on the horizon. The speck is a tiny black orb and I understand that all of the tiny black orbs that exist in the Everything, all of them, are

moveable points on a Horizon.[13]
He nods his head Yes.
This is how you will travel in the Zone, by moving the location of Points with your mind. By moving the location of Points you will be affecting their arrangement in the Zone, and affecting the movement of energy between the Points, by shifting the coordinates.
I see myself in the dis-location of the Picasso-painting-me.
Well, something like that. Certainly the Points within you but, more importantly, the Points supposedly outside of you.

The gentleman is wearing a striped robe and pointed hat. He looks like he is from the 14th or 15th century.
*I am who I am. You may call me **Umberto**.*
You must be in the proper space for this next part of the teaching. You are there now.
I feel it.
Thank you.

༄

To choose the path of travel in our dream states, whether sleeping or waking, we need to re-organize our perspective, our way of seeing. We need to loosen our notions of "reality" and be willing to create new pathways. A helpful framework that the Teachers often refer to (and Umberto uses, above) is the arrangement of Point and Zone.

 Think of every single thing, every object in the Universe, as a Point, like a dot. It can be a person, a tree, a solar system, an atom. Every "thing" is a Point. Every thing is a Point and is also simultaneously made up of Points. It is a Point made up of Points, and it is also one of many Points in something larger. Take the example of a tree. A tree is itself one thing, a Point. It is also made up of bark and limbs and leaves and sap and roots, and each

---

[13] See *Traveling Light*, p.168-180, for a lengthy discussion about the crack in the world, known as the Horizon, which can bring us closer to the wisdom of our ancestors.

of those is also made up of cells, which are made up of atoms. Every one of those things are separate Points, their own being, but they come together to make up the whole that is a tree.

In the same way, the tree itself is also one part of many larger things. It is part of a forest—a complex ecologic family of trees that feed each other and that feed other plants and animals. The tree is also part of a the larger eco-system of the Earth, sharing gases and nutrients and seeds and energy that travel all over the planet. The tree, then, is simultaneously made up of Points and is a Point and is one Point within others.

Every Point, from the sub-atomic to the intergalactic, is joined with every other Point by the space around it. The space is continuous—existing both within and around each collection of Points. The space within an atom is the same space that is within a solar system. This communal space is the "glue" between all Points, and the place where energy exchange between Points occurs. This space is called Zone.

A way to "see" Zone is to think of snow falling. Snowfall moves us emotionally not by each flake (though each flake itself is a tiny miracle), but through the great multitude of flakes swirling in concert together through space. The space between the flakes is what defines a snow cloud drifting Earthward.

Five-sense reality is focused on Points, on objects. This is how we have historically made sense of our world and maneuvered through it. The Teachers are not asking us to discard the five senses, but to move beyond them and incorporate the other senses that connect us to space, to Zone.

These other senses are not centered in the intellect, where we are used to operating. Cognitive functioning, using the brain to filter the five senses, is useful for breaking things into smaller parts and analyzing them. Using our broader sense of awareness, including intuition, moves us into new energy arrangements. These arrangements expand our consciousness to include inter-relationships within a larger context. This is where we can experience

Star Travel in other dimensions.

For most Westerners, letting go of five-sense reality can be difficult. We are geared toward the intellectual functions of sorting, organizing, labeling, and defining. The English language, for example, is about seventy percent nouns—static objects. Nouns are set Points. Only about thirty percent of our language is verbs—expressions of movement or relationship, which describe Zone. (Compare this with Native languages that are the inverse: thirty percent fixed objects and seventy percent connecting relationships.)

To travel in other dimensions, we do not have to give up the intellect or five-sense reality, we need to expand with and beyond it. In order to do this we will need to cultivate other ways of thinking and seeing and living. Cultivation takes time. It is a gradual process marked by turning the soil and unlearning, then planting new seeds and tending them.

Although it is an inner journey, we are not alone. We have the support of our ancestors, of course. There is also an undercurrent of humans, within mainstream culture, who are waking up to this way of moving. When we practice expanding our awareness beyond the five senses, in whatever way we are able, we are joining a great river of energy.

Thinking about making these energetic changes can stir up unexpected feelings, like defensiveness:

A'riquea: *You are not used to operating in this way. You are learning, yes. But what you are learning is how to be in relationship with God.*

I sense that this has something to do with letting go, something to do with allowing the good and the beautiful, the Love. Why would I feel defensive about that?

What you feel as an invasion of your space is really just the beginning of letting go of your defended boundaries. You have an idea of how your life works. That is really just an idea of how your life has worked so far. It is the way you have learned to cope and move in the world. It has brought you here. It is the way you have arrived.

And now you have entered another classroom. You are being asked to learn a new way of being. Spiritual Intimacy is about giving up the barriers that you once used to protect yourself. It is not an easy task. Being gentle with yourself is important. And, of course, not placing blame for your unease on someone else.
Maybe this defensiveness is about the need for grounding.
It could be. But it could also be about allowing another way of being. Something more fluid and unknown. Something that you do not control.

You keep allowing. You keep letting go. You keep following the sweetness. Be the butterfly dancing on the perfume of flowers. It's not a linear path. It's not a seen path. It is a sensed path. Your senses need to be open, as do your wings. Flutter. Follow. Feel.

Be forgiving with yourself. You have built these defenses over a lifetime. You can't change that overnight. What you can change is how invested you are in them. Think of it like any other difficult emotion, like anger or depression. Say, "Oh, hello, defensiveness, old friend. There you are."

Star travel doesn't land in my lap as a neat little package. There is intention-setting and patience and energy cultivation. It can be challenging to balance the needs of the physical world with the spiritual path. Do I think that I "should" be getting there faster? Am I concerned about not being "ready enough"?

Universal Wisdom: *It would be prudent to understand your energy limits. Part of the slowing down process is that you actually slow down. Not just your actions but also your thinking. Your mind is spinning all the time but not necessarily in a helpful way.*

You wonder if you are fit for this. You are more fit than ever, because some of your thinking patterns have shifted. What you find difficult is fitting this new way into your old world. It would be good to find a way to reorganize your life to match this new way of thinking. The external world is more mutable than you imagine. You know a certain way because that is what you have been trained to and it is what you have been practicing. There are people everywhere living different ways.

You are trying to use your old way because you think that is how the world works. In the West there is much attention given to focus, drive, and achievement. This is a linear thought process—that if you work hard enough in a certain way then you will be successful in a certain way. It works to some degree because it involves energy attention.

There is a free-er way to be. Trust is a big part of it. But something else comes first. First there is a knowing and accepting of the bigger universe, where many energies are working together in nonlinear ways. Art, creative function, connects with these bigger energy flows. Not energy states, because those would be static, but energy movement.

We are back to the discussion of energy Points and Zone. The benefit of being in the Zone is being bathed in the movement of energy across it. There is a constant refreshment of energy in the Zone, especially when movement is recognized and encouraged.

The gift of slowing down is that you can stop and be still. Being in constant motion yourself does not allow you to feel the Zone. Only by stepping back and allowing Zone to move through you will you be able to feel it.

Like all practice, it works best when you are able to bring it into your everyday life, when there is a continuation of what you have learned with how you live.

Stop to feel the Zone. Live in it.

Here is a lovely way to practice opening and letting go:

Begin by taking a walk in Nature by yourself. Walk along with your hands outstretched and empty, palms up and open. Walk for a distance in this way. As you walk, think about receiving gifts from the Universe into your ready palms.

We cannot be the receiver of new gifts if our hands are tightly grasping something else, if we are holding water bottles or found treasures, if we have our hands hidden in our pockets or clenched in anger. This is true of any attachment, material or emotional. Both letting go of the old and receiving the new require a relaxed and open state of reception. This difference between grasping and allowing is also the difference between holding Points and experiencing Zone.

༄

Moving into a new arrangement means that we have to let go of the old. It's not easy. Mothers know this well. Our children are constantly developing into themselves as separate beings. They are moving toward independence from the moment of conception. They first become independent of our wombs, then our breasts, then our laps, then our hand-holding. Eventually they leave our homes to make their own lives. We *want* them to become independent, to happily launch into their adult life, to carry their own children into an Earthly future which we know we will not inhabit.

We spend our entire career as parents supporting them, teaching them, guiding them, getting them ready for this moment. All along the way, we can't help but be a step or two behind their progress. We just get something figured out and they're on to the next stage. For the successful parent this is a constant, ongoing process of letting go.

The process of letting go is similar for spiritual travelers. If we want to build new areas of spiritual evolution into our lives, we will need to constantly practice letting go of our old ways.

A'riquea: *It is more difficult to shift when someone is working to maintain a predictable path. Then everything that occurs must be made to fit that fixed way of seeing and Being. There is not a recipe or an exercise workout that will change this. A decision has to be made, a choice. The choice is between being in the moment and being out of the moment.*

The intellect is not in the moment. It takes over because it is basing its action on the past, and assumes that the future can only be the same as the past—that it is not mutable. The emotional self can act in the moment if it is freed of the judgment of the intellect. When the emotional self is acting in the moment, new ways can be created.

Humans easily judge the emotional self as being "childish," because it has less regard for consequences than the intellect. But a child-like quality is exactly what is needed to create new ways. Child-like quality values curiosity and adventure and let's-see-what-happens. It does not pre-judge outcomes. Practice being in the moment, no matter what it is that you are doing.

Letting go, creating new pathways, practicing Star Travel, only occurs with the energy input of our intention. The loosening of our hold on five-sense reality is a choice. It is a choice supported by our ancestors.

Universal Wisdom: *You have the opportunity to practice doing things a different way. Be very clear on this—it is a choice. The choice is to fall back on old patterns and repeat them, or to see the patterns and choose to try something else.*

The Something Else is a trial. Hopefully, you will be able to tell what works and what doesn't. The way to tell is the vibration. The vibration in your body. It is possible to feel safe and secure because you are given freedom and control. It is also possible to feel this way because you are shut down. One feels like an opening, the other like a closing. If you are turning away, you are closing down. If you are turning toward, you are opening.

Life is complex. Remember the discussion of the blueprint, with the matrix built on that framework.[14] The beauty of Life is the vibration that occurs within the framework of the matrix. It is not the matrix itself, although that is necessarily part of it. But it has more to do with the vibration created by the existence of the matrix, and that vibration is generated by the soul within. Shining a light on the soul

---

[14] The blueprint and matrix are discussed in *Traveling Light*, p. 36-44. Basically, we come into the world with a blueprint based on the specific circumstances of our genetics, epigenetics, and birth. As we navigate the world in a physical body we generate a framework, or matrix, of energy structures over our lifetime. The matrix is defined by the energy vibrating within that structure. We are responsible for its creation.

path creates an energy that allows the matrix to vibrate, to resonate at a clearer frequency. The spirit-fed life illuminates the soul path, increases its brilliance. It burns away the barbs, the sticking points, that reduce flow and freedom. It allows more Being.

We want you to know that we are here for you, we are supporting this kind of growth and change. Enter into healing with the support of the Universe. It is in everyone's best interest that you see your pain and injury in the light of growth and healing, that you continue to move, that you continue to expand, and that you fill the space created with the energy of Love and Light. This is your purpose. It is why you are here.

Making these changes will upend our learned notions about how we move through the world.

A'riquea: *This next part of your life will be about a different kind of production. You are going to be manifesting that which is unseen. You are going to be helping to bring something new into existence. It is actually ancient, but it will be new in this Time. Sometimes you are going to feel lost, because that is what it is like to create something. It seems like it comes out of nothing. Really, it comes from everything. It is just that you will be organizing the parts in a new way, a rearranging. That is how there will be more Space for all that you do. Because the previous arrangement has been distorted.*

It is a good time to be at home, rebuilding the core. It is not wrong. There is time to use to your advantage. Be happy for all the life you have.

Grace, purpose, humor.
And Love.

Letting go of our old ways and creating new ones is not a smooth or direct pathway. Creativity requires us to be open to ideas and experiences that we haven't seen before and may not understand. We need to be able to free our minds and accept these things without judgement. As preparation for dimensional travel, we have to learn to tolerate the absurd.

One day **Aniimaakii** came to me and took me by the hand.

With his other hand sweeping across the sky, he shows me a giant rainbow. Then he points to my torso, where I see the many rainbows of all my cells, like wind chimes tinkling in the wind. I see the same rainbows in my body as I see in the sky.

Aniimaakii encourages me to choose a color. Purple comes to mind and I see Aniimaakii smile and nod. I feel calm and accepting, curious for a new experience. I go to the purple and allow it to gently enter me.

I am standing upright in a white space. The purple is a thick liquid, like paint. My being is open and the purple is pouring in a stream into the top of my head. It is filling me. It pools under my eyes. It travels down my throat. It has entered every alveolar sac in my lungs. When I breathe it moves rhythmically with my breath, up and down my spine and up along the back of my head, circulating back again into the chakra at the top of my crown. It is gently spraying out of my ears. Aniimaakii has his hand over his mouth, trying to hide a grin. This makes me smile, too. I have to be willing to be foolish, to look silly.

Creation is filling me with beauty and wonder. The skin on my face is purple. The irises of my eyes are bright red, the pupils white. There is a red cord of energy looping from the front of my chest, between my legs, and up the back of my chest. There are bright green fronds of energy growing out from the center of my belly, like fingers, and stretching around in a circle to attach to my lower back. Ah, my arms. They are black feathered wings. The purple is continuously pumping through my lungs, through my spine, through my crown. My heart is a molten yellow orb, too bright to look at.

Aniimaakii is looking away, his shoulders shaking with laughter. I guess I don't care if you are making fun of me. I am enjoying this process. Maybe this is what my spirit body looks like, when it is attached to my physical body?

There, finally, I am seeing my feet. They are blue, webbed, flippers. When I ask, What is this clown suit? Aniimaakii's eyebrows shoot up in surprise and concern, as if I have blasphemed. Yet I am still sitting here in this colorful spirit body. I am more than willing to wear this. I don't understand how it is being shown to me and I am also being ridiculed for wearing it. There is something very funny here. I want to laugh out loud. I don't really feel the need to figure this out. It seems like none of my business right now. There is a beaded feather attached to the back of my hair. Even though my arms are black-feathered wings, I have hands, with bright red painted nails, and these hands are doing the typing.

I am all of these pieces put together. I come from all of these places. I came from all of these places before I came here. I wonder if there is something I need to be looking for, to add, while I am here, that I will need where I am going. Aniimaakii nods his head Yes. His arm is reaching across his body, his finger pointing to something behind me to my left. I turn to look and see a giant golden dragon-lion. My mind wants to discard this image as just a remnant from living with a cat for the last three days. But maybe that is why the cat is with me, to help me make this connection? The dragon-lion has come to sit beside me. It is huge, at least three times larger than I am. It is just sitting with me. It looks over at me and draws back when it sees my colored spirit body. Maybe the dragon-lion is a spirit body too?

Aniimaakii is laughing and pointing now. At us. Ok, Aniimaakii, Let's see *your* spirit body. Now he has his chin in his hand, thinking. He shakes his head No. I ask, Are you a woman? He looks surprised again, but not concerned. He is thoughtful.

What a strange interaction this is. I have trouble believing that it is real, just because there are so many odd parts to it that I don't understand. Could I be making all this up? I wonder what will happen if I go back to the beginning, where Aniimaakii brought me to the rainbow. Now I am rolling in the colors of the rainbow. There are fun little zaps of energy in all of them, like tiny static electric shocks. Then Aniimaakii motions for me to come back to him. He points to his side and I am standing there. He is a grown man and I am a girl child. He kneels in front of me. His eyes are very gentle. He talks to me with his eyes:

This is the way you are going to travel. We will be taking you. You will have to get used to the absurd, for everything will seem absurd in the new context. It is right to not take things personally, to not react with ego. You must be able to hold only spirit energy and leave the ego behind. A certain amount of stability is going to be required. You were practicing today.

I feel small and innocent. I have a feather in my hand. We walk away together.

In the previous vision, my job was just to accept the absurd without judgement. Although teachings are usually gentle like this, other times they evidence in jarring, even traumatic, ways. One night I was driving home. It was right around dusk and snowing hard. Out of nowhere there was a very loud bang. I thought something in my engine had blown up. But there was no smoke and no change in the car's performance. I looked in all my mirrors. I saw feathers stuck on the driver's side of the car and a large black ball in the road behind me. I was stunned. A very large bird had struck the side of my car.

  I kept driving. I was not thinking very well, over-tired from work. I wondered if I should turn around and look for the bird. I got all the way home, still wondering if I should go back. By then it was very dark and snowing harder, and many other vehicles would have already driven by that spot.

  I looked at my car. The bird had struck the post between the driver's and the passenger's door, basically right where I was sitting. There were a few under-feathers that looked like they were from a hawk or golden eagle, and spattered blood and flesh. I felt guilty—for harming the bird, even though it was not intentional. I also felt guilty that the bird had made an offering to me, of feathers, and I had not accepted it. I said a prayer and made an offering to the bird. As I walked away from my offering tree, I suddenly remembered another time that a large bird had struck my car.

  Back then, I was still working as a nurse, and for some reason I was driving to work that day instead of taking the bus. There was a road kill on the highway and it was covered with birds getting a meal, including four or five bald eagles. The feast was on the other side of the road, and there was a whole lane of pavement plus the ditch between me and the birds. Suddenly there was a loud bang and a bald eagle was splayed across my windshield, its wings outstretched and its black golden eye looking directly into mine. I slowed down but did not stop because there were many large predators there. The eagle was not in the road. I could not see where it had gone. There was a powdery imprint of the eagle on the windshield, outlining every feather, that stayed there for several weeks after.

I was rattled to my core. When I got to work I made an offering at the council trees. I went to an elder and asked what I should do, spiritually. He suggested I make an offering, which I had already done. He said the eagle had probably come to me as a messenger. A few days later, I had my first chemo infusion and suffered a traumatic brain injury. I was never able to go back to work. My world turned upside down and was never the same again.

And now another eagle had struck my car, giving me a heads up that a big change was coming. I kept re-hearing that big bang. I was worried. All I could do was breathe and live well, open myself to whatever opportunity might appear. I wondered if there was anything for me to know:

Universal Wisdom: *We are paying attention to what you have been asking for. We are working the channels as best we can. There is nothing to be afraid of.*

I have to stop and just breathe into that. Nothing to be afraid of.

This is a difficult thing to describe, because it involves other actors, so there is no way of knowing just how it will play out. The best thing to do is practice patience and keep moving the gift. Keep helping yourself into the New World. Live Life. Don't hold back. Be the Change.

All of the lessons you have been learning will come to bear. It may feel like a calamity. All the more reason to stay the course. Be Free. One day at a time. And make each day a good day.

The Covid-19 pandemic hit one month later. The entire world was thrown into a blanket toss of unprecedented and lasting change. It challenged us to reevaluate and reinvent every aspect of our lives—personally, communally, and globally.

For decades, my Teachers had been telling me about a coming shift in cosmic consciousness, a shift both within and beyond the world as we know it. I could not even imagine what that would look like. They said the change would be so great that we would not be able to choose *if,* only *how,* we would participate.

A'riquea: *This is a difficult situation, isn't it? You will need to find some other coping mechanisms. You have decided that you know how the world works. You know what your own experience in the past has been, and how you reacted to it. You do not know all of the possible situations and outcomes. By claiming to know, you are closing off all of the other possibilities.*

You have to let go of knowing in order to move forward. You decide how you want your present to resonate. With the jarring hardness of being chained to an out-dated definition? Or with the wonder-full freedom of opening to what's next.

Opening to what's next requires a certain amount of trust. Trust that it's going to work out, not necessarily the way I might envision it, but the way it needs to. I've had many events in my life that appeared as traumatic but eventually led me to the next leg of my journey.

A difficult birth led me to heal childhood trauma. A painful divorce with small children opened the way for the beginning of my book-writing process. Cancer burned all of my ego identities down to the ground until only my spiritual life remained, not only beautifully intact but strengthened. Financial distress brought me to a rustic life in closer contact with Nature. Through all of these changes, channeling, with its teachings and transcendence, prepared me to accept the opportunities embedded in change. The pandemic created those kinds of opportunities for everyone simultaneously.

The Library Man: *This is a beginning, of sorts. Yes, you have come through much change to get here. So it is a fruition, in a way. But that* *transformation is now behind you. And it couldn't have been any other way. We do not need to dwell on that.*

What we want to focus on is what needs to Be going forward. You have had a certain expectation about how the process works, that you follow these certain channels and then you end up down the road where you want to be. It is not going to be like that. You are just going to have to be open to what's next. And what does Being Open mean?

Being Open means that there is a clearing of the structures that have been built on the blueprint. The blueprint is still there, it is the foundation. But the structures that once held your life in place have been dismantled. You do not have the same connections to family—your children and your parents have moved on. You do not have the same connections to work, or social life, or the material world—all of the things that keep you in a box. Now you will become someone else.

You are thinking about how people change over their lifetime. You are no longer the child you once were, even though you carry those experiences. But those experiences can be changed into something else by processing the events in a different way. And this is how you grow and evolve. So you are not that child, even though your physical body was built on the blueprint of that first expression.

So now you are to become something else. Some of this you have control over. You can decide what actions to take, who to interact with, how to utilize your time. All of that brings you to the next thing. Of course, we cannot tell you what that next thing is. It is something you have to discover. Letting go of the past helps free you to become this next thing.

The qualities you want to bring to this are curiosity and delight. We want you to enjoy what comes next. If it feels like responsibility or drudgery, then it is not the next thing. You have much practice in being responsible, so that is not an issue. You have less experience in delight. This is your next path.

I am thinking about Marie Kondo, the Netflix queen of organizing, and how her process not only clears material clutter but also brings people back in touch with what brings them joy.

You have this opportunity now. We want you to focus on joy. There is a specific reason to do this. Responsibility brings things into a Point. Joy brings your energy into the expansiveness of Space. It is that simple. The Next World is in the experience of Space. You will need to organize your cells to align them with this context, and then you will see what can happen. As you know, it can not be thought into existence, it has to be experienced.

I feel it now. It is not just Space, although that is where it occurs. The expansion of being in Space *with positive energy* is an expansion multiplier.

It is like the fun house of mirrors—it can go on and on and on, infinitely. At some point you will enter this infinity. For now, you will need to practice expanding in Space. And you do this by discovering and cultivating Joy and Delight.

What a great assignment!

Of course, it will not be as easy as you think, but yes, it should be en-joy-able.

Thank you. I have been looking forward to the journey to the Next World. I assumed that that is why I was doing so much clearing out. But I had to idea where I was going.

You still do not.

Of course.

You must maintain yourself in the Unknown.

Space. Expansion. Stop trying to nail it down.

And stop thinking about it so much. This has to do with experience.

Cellular vibration. Resonance.

Even those are just words. Focus on feelings.

Keep coming back. We have missed you.

I am starting again.

Another beginning.

~ 2 ~

Destination Unknown

Westerners prefer to organize the world intellectually—by analyzing things and placing them in neatly-defined categories, and we tend to discount anything that does not fit that model. This favoring of rational thinking comes, however, at the expense of wisdom available from other sources. Transcendence is a way to experience consciousness and acquire knowledge. It provides information through bodily sensations of energy.

To *transcend* means to go beyond a limit. Spiritual transcendence means expanding our energy beyond the known world into the unknown. This expansion is not something that can be done through the intellect, by figuring it out, or by willing it to happen. It's something that is felt. It is an experience. It's similar to love, which is impossible to describe using words alone because love is a feeling. Like love, transcendence is the experience of an energy sensation.

Gaining an understanding of transcendence requires practice. You can come to it through meditation, martial arts, music, art, nature, ritual, or spiritual exploration. With continued practice this sensation is recorded as a memory in your body, and you can return to it over and over. Then it becomes a resource for balanced living and spiritual evolution.

We can think of transcendence as a journey. Our starting point for that journey is the physical world, the five sense reality that anchors our daily lives in our physical body. With spiritual travel our journey's destination is the Infinite Universe. Leaving what we know in order to enter the unknown, shifting our energy toward infinity, can sometimes feel disorienting. This is because we are adjusting our sense of what is "real."

Universal Wisdom: *We are interested in your development as a spiritual expression. It is not in our job description to decide what is "real." That is a perceptive process that resides in the individual. You are the one who has to decide if this perspective is deranged or not. If you choose to think you are crazy, by cultural standards, then you will be. Another option is to know that you are traveling a different path than your surface culture. It is going to feel disconnected, because you are.*

What we want you to know about this is that you have more control than you think. The control, however, comes in the ability to let go.

Letting go is not about letting the ego run rampant, it's about letting go of functioning through the ego only, so we can move with spirit. These terms can be confusing.

The True Self is your genetic heritage, the You that was created in the joining of DNA at conception. It is a history and a blueprint, which is then built on to create a Self. The building of this matrix occurs through the experience of Life Force, the pressures and freedoms of Living.

Spirit is a layer of energy that infuses Life Force with Meaning. It creates connections and relationships with other Beings by recognizing Life Force in them. Spirit is a shared experience, a relational energy that runs through multiple dimensions simultaneously. That is why it feels open and expansive. Your energy needs to be open and expansive to connect with Spirit. It is a two-way exchange of movement.

Ego is energy that is linked to the physical plane only. Of course, the physical plane is energized by many other dimensions, and the ego can sense this, but its perspective is limited to the physical plane. That is also the limit of its function. As you know, it has a place, and an important place, in the preservation of the physical body. These three energy bodies [True Self, Spirit, Ego] *work in concert. Sometimes the music is beautiful. It can also be out of tune, creating discord and disorder.*

Realize that this all requires practice. Your current culture feeds Ego and attempts to ignore Spirit. Most people have some awareness of the limits of this arrangement, they are aware of Spirit in themselves and also in others. You can help them to become comfortable talking about this. Be a model for the "new" normal.

What I want to model is acceptance. As I've been told before, "Don't be afraid that something is wrong, be aware that something is different." What would be an example of these different energy bodies?

The True Self is the original self, the You before Life happened to you. It is the Tree of Being, and its roots are the Soul, grounded in the Universe. Spirit is the water and the air and the sunlight for this Tree of Being.

Ego is the tree, the physical manifestation, the bark and the trunk and the limbs. It is an expression of living on the physical plane. Of course it is infused with Life Force. It has to be in order to be living. Ego is the hardened exterior that allows for survival. It is also the hardened exterior that creates an identity, an appearance, how we think we appear to others. Birds in the trees are spirit messengers. Their message is their movement, which is a reminder of the flow of spiritual energy.

We are like trees in a forest. Our 'hardened exterior' is our ego, the 'me' who exists on the physical plane. Our ego is attached to everything we cannot change about our appearance—things that help us belong to groups (like "birches" or "pines," and "saplings" or "old-growth"). These ego-attachments also set us apart from others. If we are trees, then we are *not* ferns or ants or oceans. We are quite familiar with our identity, with our own physical manifestation of the tree of life, because it houses our experience on Earth.

Rarely do we incorporate awareness of all the other energy connections that are required to produce and maintain this physical presence. From moment to moment every day of the year, a tree relies on other trees and plants, on soil and insects and microbes. A tree shares energy with air and water and sunlight. A tree is infused with Life Force, with the eternal energy movement of the Great Mystery. The physical appearance of the tree is but one expression of Life and the Universe, of Spirit and Soul. Our own physical manifestation, our ego, is also but one expression of our Being.

My ego is my visible physical expression. My spirit is all of the life-energies that fuel this physical expression. My soul is all of the energies that I have ever been and ever will be. The energies of my ego, spirit and soul all exist simultaneously in one space. Which of these energies I function with is determined by where I focus my attention.

I had a dream that helped me understand these energies, how they occupy the same space, and how to shift between them. In the dream, I saw the words: "The process of Me, in the Unlit Dark."

"The process of Me" is the Life Journey of Ego, of Me. But what is the "Unlit Dark"? It sounds like the part of living that occurs beyond the light of day, in the places we can't see. It's a sensation, the movement of energy, without the usual five senses input. Does it describe the intuitive, psychic, spiritual realm?

A'riquea: *It describes the part of you that communicates with other worlds, usually without your awareness, But that is always happening. There is a trick you play on yourself to reduce your awareness of it. That trick is to bring the five sense world to the foreground and hold it there. If you want to transcend, you will need to let go of this. You will need more balance—letting the darkness become part of your everyday life.*

Yes, humans tend to describe the dark parts as the evil parts. This is part of the trick that is used to keep the darkness away—filling it with monsters and danger. The darkness, like the light, is neither good nor bad. It is a space where energy moves. Good and Bad are relative movements of energy. Just like the discussion of oppression in the first book,[15] everything is relative.

---

[15] *Grandmother Dreams*, p. 78-82.

How does the quality of the darkness differ from the light? If there are two things there must be some difference.
The Light is part of the physical world. It is what you see. Of course, the divisions are not really black and white. But it provides a way to think about it. The dark is all that is felt without knowing. It is the mystery, the other side, what is across the veil, another way of being that is more fluid and changeable.
If the Light is the physical world, then the Dark would be the Dream World?
The Dark is the not-physical.
Think about what it is like to be in a dark room, a room without any light. Place yourself there.
It is completely dark, no light. I cannot move around, because I will run into things. There is nowhere to go, anyway. I am here. Sitting quietly. I become more and more aware of my own body, my breath moving in and out, my heart beating. I am aware of a slow pulsing of energy, energy that is rhythmically expanding and contracting through me. I am aware of my skin, which is some kind of boundary between me and not me. In the absence of any other input, I am the process of Me.....in the unlit dark........
[A'riquea is smiling.]

There is a simple exercise that you can do yourself to create this shift in energy attention. You will need a fully darkened room with no light at all, none. The room also needs to be quiet, with no sound intrusion. If your room is not dark or quiet enough, a closet may work. A good time to practice this is very late at night when most of the outer world is sleeping.

Set a timer for 20-30 minutes. This prevents your brain from constantly engaging in guessing how much time has gone by. You will be done when the timer goes off.

Sit in a comfortable position *with your eyes open*. Let your body become used to the dark. Allow it. Relax into it. Become aware of your breathing. Become aware of your body's energy.

Feel the sensations that are available when you are aware

and alert but vision and hearing are not guiding your experience. Let your awareness rest in your inner processes, the energy movement of existing. Let your awareness rest in your outer environment, the energy movement of living. Let it all flow and Be.

This is a way to practice energy awareness.

After doing this dark-room exercise several times, I began to be more aware of light at different times of day. I was lying awake early one morning looking around the room. The blue light of dawn was just barely beginning to filter in. I was keenly aware that this was the exact same room I had been lying in the night before, when it was completely dark and I could see nothing, but now I could see everything.

It's the light that makes things seem different, that makes my awareness shift. It's the same with consciousness. In the light, I am aware of physical objects and my relationship to them. In the unlit darkness, I am aware of myself and my body in relationship to energy. I am the same person, my environment is the same, but the location of my awareness changes.

This is how two worlds, the Physical World and the Dream World, can be present simultaneously. My consciousness changes when I shift my attention between them. Transcending does not require that I leave my body, it just means that I experience myself in another realm.

These realms are present simultaneously. One does not "go away" while we are in the other. They are all there, all the time. **Eagle Brother**, my Teacher, came to show me how this is possible.

We were at pow-wow, which I love. There, I am detached from city life and the world of technology. I am immersed in the sound of the drum, the heartbeat, at least ten hours a day. I am dancing and turning the circle of life. I am connecting with community, with all of its traditional beauty and quirky dysfunction. During this time I am cultivating appreciation and gratitude. By the time pow-wow is over, I am bursting with Love—Love for everything on the planet, for all things seen and unseen.

At the end of one pow-wow Eagle Brother came to me and I traveled with him in the Spirit World. He pointed to the horizon out on The Big Lake. Together, we traveled to the line of the horizon, and then through it, where we came into another world. It was the world of the starry sky, the Universe. We were floating in it. We had no bodies—we were loosely organized points of colored lights. He was showing me our spirit bodies, showing me how we interact as spirits. I felt light and happy. I could feel him smiling. Then we went through another horizon, beyond the Universe, into God. There was only blinding white light there, and our spirit bodies dissolved into that light. We ceased to be ourselves or our spirits and joined the One With All. All of this occurred while I was inhabiting a physical body on Earth.

Eagle Brother showed me how we can be in multiple worlds simultaneously. We are the physical form that we see on Earth, *and* we are the expanded spirit bodies of the Universe, *and* we are One With God. We are all of these things, all at once. Where we focus our attention determines where we will "be."

∞

When we expand our consciousness beyond the body into the Unknown, into the Mystery, this crossing of an invisible zone is often referred to as The Veil. This interface is not a fixed line. It is not an exact location. "Crossing The Veil" just describes a rearrangement of our energy and perception which resembles the pulling back of a curtain—as if we are lifting a veil from our awareness.

This veil, the division between two worlds, is not something we can prove scientifically. Science uses rational thinking to break things down into smaller and smaller pieces to measure and study them. Trying to do this to define the veil would destroy what we were trying to study. As Bernd Heinrich, a well-known researcher of raven behavior, notes: "We'll never find proof for the existence of consciousness by picking the animal apart, or by looking at its parts in isolation. That's like trying to understand the caching behavior of ravens by grinding them up, examining ever smaller parts down to the molecules, and studying them through the laws for physics and chemistry. That's backwards.....Consciousness is not *a* thing. It is a continuum without boundaries."[16]

Consciousness is a continuum without boundaries. Although the veil itself is often referred to as a boundary, it is not something we can pinpoint and locate. It is a shift in attention and energy. We can begin to sense what the two "sides" of this transformation might be by understanding them as mirror images of each other. The mirror images on either side of the veil are the Physical World and the Dream World:

Physical World	Dream World
Ego, Five Senses	Spirit, Beyond Five Senses
Known, Seen	Unknown, Unseen
Form, Sensation	Not Form, Sensing
Brain, Intellect	Mind, Awareness
Labeling, Analyzing	Inclusive, No Explanation
Scientific, Factual	Feeling, Experiential
Linear, Rational	Encompassing, Intuitive
Rules, Control, Attachment	Creativity, Allowing, Surrender
Immediacy, Time	Ever Present, Timelessness
Points, Objects	Zone, Space

It is convenient to envision the two sides of the veil as separate. Of course, they are not. Thinking about them as mirror images is just a way to understand the continuum of consciousness. The mirror

---

[16] *Mind of the Raven, Investigations and Adventures with Wolf-Birds* (Harper Collins, 1999), p. 339.

images are really parts of a whole that include both. Like Yin and Yang, they reflect each other. One reminds us of the complimentary characteristics of the other.

> "The property of light is discerned in dependence on darkness. The property of beauty is discerned in dependence on the unattractive. The property of the dimension of the infinitude of space is discerned in dependence on form."
> ~ *Sattadhatu Sutta, SN 14.11*

If either side of the veil are mirror images, then what is the mirror? We are the mirror. We are the channel which is expressing either side of the veil. What we experience is based on where we place our awareness, where we rest our attention. Our purpose is not to fix ourselves on one end or the other, or to alternate between the two, but to integrate both into one.

We think of our bones, for instance, as our skeleton. Bones are what is left after all of our flesh has returned to the Earth. That's what is meant by 'bare bones'—the exposure of the central structure, the most lasting framework of an animal body. When we are actively in human form, however, the hollow places inside our bones are also the place where our blood, the life-giving fluid for all the rest of our body, is created.

A'riquea: *Bones are the place where Life Force is generated—in the marrow of the bones.*

It's where our blood originates. That's an interesting parallel: one of the hardest substance in the human body is, at its center, soft and spongy. So bones are both rock-like, and soft. Solid *and* mysterious. [A'riquea is smiling.] *They work in concert with each other.*

This is the essence of God, creating a form which you know as your body, which is both a physical form and a spiritual vessel. It is a Home for the spirit while traveling on the physical plane. This is a once-in-a-lifetime opportunity, literally. It is the marriage of Yin and Yang, of hard and soft, of action and intuition.

They are complimentary. Your purpose is not to alternate

between the two—that would be duality. Your purpose is to integrate, to be both and neither. It takes practice, and awareness. Practice the awareness.

A practice which embodies this awareness is a standing meditation called *Form–Feel–Fill–Heal*.[17]

Balance gently on both legs, with soft knees, your feet hip-distance apart and one foot slightly ahead of the other. Put both of your arms out in front of you, palms up, and give thanks for the many dimensions of which you are made.

Start with the awareness of *Form*, which is your physical identity. Your form is defined by all the space around you, by everything up to the boundary of your skin. Breathe deeply and increase your awareness of the opportunities gifted you in this physical body. Give thanks for your Form.

Next, honor the vibration of *Feel*, which is all of the energy starting with the boundary of your skin and moving inward, including the tissues and blood and emotional sensations of living. All of it is in constant, internal motion, working together like a symphony of many instruments. Breathe deeply, and increase your awareness of this flow. Give thanks for the gift of your ability to Feel.

Now honor *Fill*. Fill yourself with the white light of the Universe, which is generated in your bones, beaming out Life Force to fuel your existence. Breathe deeply and increase your awareness of this resource. Honor and give thanks for being Filled with Life Force.

Finally, honor *Healing*, through the grounding of the Earth and the freedom of the sky. Both of these energies are connecting in your body, constantly flowing up and down your spine, bringing you into balance. Breathe deeply and increase your awareness of this balanced connection. Give thanks and honor this Healing.

Finish by welcoming your Spirit home and honoring your

---

[17] Adaptation of a practice I learned from Wendy Palmer.

presence. Into this space of honoring, give thanks for the part of you that is your Spirit Moving. Say aloud: "I welcome my Spirit Home." Give thanks for all the Spirit Helpers and Ancestor Families that support you. Then focus your attention on on each word as you say: " I. Choose. This. Moment."

༄

A balanced life requires the integration of both the physical and the spiritual—both sides of the veil. Focusing solely on the body is harmful, but neither can we divorce ourselves from it. The body is our living vehicle for opportunity. It allows us to feel the vibration of transcendence in physical form. Our goal is to balance the physical with the non-physical.

At times in my life I've become unbalanced and needed to purposefully create a space to address this. Once, I went on a four day solo retreat at a rustic cabin, on a remote lake accessible only by canoe. I went there to reconnect with Being.

To reconnect with Being, I had to disconnect from doing. I had to step away from projects and staying busy, from jumping up to do the next thing. I removed myself from checking the time and temperature, from reacting to deadlines. There was no phone service. I didn't want to have to respond to others' needs or care about the news.

The first full day was a struggle. It stretched loooong. I was bored, and it was educational observing myself cope with that. I craved a cigarette even though I've never smoked. I thought of smoking pot, considered drinking, was tempted to make coffee—all chemical means to avoid ownership of my inner life. I did not have my usual paper piles to deal with or phone calls to make, no work email, no internet. There were no home repair projects, no laundry or grocery shopping. I did not bring any books to fill up my time and distract me. And the dense woods, thick with mosquitoes, had no hiking trails.

That left a lot of sitting around, laying around, thinking, trying not to think. I wondered how many days it would take for my mind to run through every likely groove. I practiced patience, relaxation, unknowing, allowing. I stared into space. I did a whole lot of Nuthin'.

Planning, managing, doing, linear functioning—these are all activities that Western culture not only rewards but encourages to the exclusion of other parts of ourselves. We are given little license for timelessness, free-association, or being. I was sitting on the shore of the lake thinking about this split, when a loon surfaced about 60 feet away. She called several times, her beautiful flute flowing across the water and resonating on the rocks. A stunning song. Through my mind she gave me these words about air and water, about doing and being:

The Loon: *You must dive deep for your food. This is what will nourish you. At certain times you must take to the air, to travel to the next lake, to migrate for the season. But that movement is always to the next place of food and nourishment, which is deep in the water, which is deep in the Universe.*

If you spend all of your time in the air, you will not be nourished, you will not thrive and reproduce your energy. You will become weak. You know this. Pay attention to where you are traveling. In the air, in the water, they are both important but for different reasons.

You also cannot stay in the deep water. You must come up for air, you must surface to survive. You see, it is all important, but in different ways. This is the path for you—balance and awareness.

I am thinking that one way I could help myself is to schedule time in the Dream World, the Spirit World. I cannot just hope to find time for this among all the other things that are getting my attention. I need to do something like this retreat on a regular basis, not wait until I'm burned out. Each of my days need to have this component, in at least equal energy allotments. It is helpful to think of this as air and water, and consider what being in either element brings to my life.

It is important to enjoy each element, not just use it for practical purposes. If you are not enjoying it then it is not worth doing.

I tend to think that there are a lot of tasks that just need to get done.

The list grows and grows, until it takes over my time and energy. That is giving the Planner too much authority.
The Planner is like the ego. It carries out the tasks that you give it. It takes energy and moves it in a linear way. The Dreamer expands to hold space and allow new energy to come in. You are both of these, and you are also bigger than these. You are the Yin and the Yang of this energy movement, and you are the whole. When you focus only on the doing, you are out of balance.

Be the circle, and everything in it. Then see the circle in the bigger picture, outside of Time. Decide to occupy Space, not Time.
Just then the loon flapped its wings along the surface of the water and lifted itself into the sky, heading for the next lake.

It is our body that allows us to feel the vibration of transcendence in physical form. Our purpose in transcendence is to travel into the Dream World and then to bring back the learning we experience there, while continuing to em*body* those vibrations. We do not leave our body to experience these vibrations, we allow our body to incorporate them.

I was walking through a construction site when an eagle feather laid itself across my path. The feather was a little muddy, but the downy ring along the bottom was still fluffy around the shaft. I had stopped at the site to get a better look at a bald eagle in the river below. It was no accident that there was a feather there. It's easy to say that it's just a coincidence that I was walking by and found it. That's one way to look at it.

Another way to see it is as a powerful message. I have been reminded over and over of my purpose in life—Thunderbird medicine. Sometimes I don't know what that means. The Thunderbird is connected with spirituality, with bringing the spiritual into the physical. I often meet the Thunderbird at my Spirit Place far out in the woods. Two of my Spirit Names are related to Thunderbirds. An elder mentioned to me that this time in the world is the seventh fire, and it is the time of the Thunderbird. I am consistently drawn to the Thunderbird. I think it describes the kind of work I am doing with these books. I can't define it but it is all there, this flow of energy around spiritual healing and making deeper connections.

I feel energized when I talk about this. It is my purpose. Everything else is just a distraction. Being gifted with that feather is another reminder of where I need to focus. Where I *want* to focus. It is so easy to get off-track.

I am holding that eagle feather now. Its power is almost overwhelming. Tears are filling my eyes. I see the bald eagle above me, lifting off from a high tree branch. I hear its piercing call, echoing over the forest. The eagle has turned in flight and flown straight at me, talons out. It is clawing in my brain, under my skull. The bird stands before me, white head cocked to one side, yellow eyes surveying me. It is speaking, its beak open. I see the back of its throat and enter its mouth. I am inside the eagle as it lifts off again, with me inside. She spreads her wings wide and takes off into the blue sky.

We are flying now, above the land. The rustling forest and the sparkling lake are below. She calls out, the eagle's call. Many eagles are lifting up from the trees, taking flight with us, wheeling and circling in the clear fall sky, the sun shimmering on the lake far below. The birds are coming together, circling and calling. More eagles keep lifting out of the trees below, joining us. The sun is warm on our dark feathers. The wind is holding us high, supporting our wings. Our calls ring out, echoing through the world. The world is vibrating with these calls. The Earth is vibrating and the lake moves with this hum of energy, its pattern evident on the surface of the water. The sun dances off of these patterns and throws sparkles into the air. The air supports these sparkles, they are the rainbow prisms I have seen in other visions. They are the energy of thought and action and Life. I am entering one of these rainbow sparkles. I am an eagle flying into a giant rainbow.

As my wings cut the surface of the rainbow I become millions of tiny rainbow sparkles. My body is made of them. And each of those rainbows within me has an eagle flying through it, becoming millions more rainbow sparkles. It is an infinite process, like looking into a hall of mirrors. On and on and on. It never stops. There is no end. There is no beginning. There are endless rainbow sparkles and eagles flying through rainbows, making more sparkles with more eagles flying through them.

Suddenly there is a burst of blinding white light, and I am in the presence of God. My entire body is consumed by the brilliant light. Everything everywhere is consumed by the light. The Light. The Light of Love. It is vibrating in every cell and atom of my body, in all of the space between every cell and every atom. I am humming with energy, energy that is organizing my being into wholeness and beauty. Dark feathers are sprouting on my fingers. Then on my arms and my body. I am the Thunderbird. I am the Power of the Universe expressed in physical form. I transpire across all dimensions instantly and simultaneously.

Aniimaakii: *This is where we bring our energies together, to move the spiritual into the physical and the physical into the spiritual. It is a movement of energy. This is movement in the Zone, the holding together of all that needs to Be, not in a static Point, but in constant and steady motion. This is the vibration, the vibrancy, the Living, the Oneness, the Everything, constantly refreshed through movement and Divine Intention.*

We begin with the Feather. The Feather alone does not fly. The Thunderbird does not fly without feathers. This is the interdependence of All Things. You are not the Thunderbird. You are Thunderbird Energy. You are the movement of Life in every Breath. The Breath moves into your body and out of your body, connecting your inside with your outside. The air you breathe is constantly moving, in and out of you, in and out of others, in and around others, all over the Planet. See yourself in motion, the Thunderbird Energy in motion. Tend to that which is Wise, and Beautiful and Helpful. Bring this Energy into the World in the Way that you Fly. The way that you Move. The way that you Are. Share the Gifts of Awareness and Love. Share your Knowing. Be the Thunderbird. In the Sky of the World. In the Rainbows. Be the Thunderbird.

Go In Peace.

I feel the energy moving in me. It is swishing back and forth, like water in a glass before it reaches equilibrium. So we are to move energy back and forth. Not just focus on putting our energy across the veil, into the Spirit World, but to also bring it back from the Spirit World into the Physical World. To keep that energy refreshed by *moving* it, moving it back and forth, and being in the space of that movement, refreshed by its movement.

∞

Traveling in the Spirit World is something that changes us. This is something that the Teachers are encouraging—not just for our personal benefit but for the continued growth of the Universe. It is important for evolution.

The Library Man: *This is something we are working towards. It cannot be felt until you have actually experienced it. There is an opening you must pass through. Like the passage when you are born in human form. It is a birth, into the next layer of consciousness. It is not a new dimension, per se, because all dimensions are present simultaneously. But it is a world that your awareness has not yet experienced in human form.*

It is one of many. Your mind understands the importance of this. There is going to be a change in the human world, and it will be important for some of the learning of human form to be transferred into this Next World. It is a place you will experience, and then you will bring this learning along with you.

The importance of the human experience is that it occurs in a physical body, so the learning becomes not only knowledge but also vibration. It affects cellular and atomic levels in a way that non-physical learning cannot.

I'm thinking of how, once I have experienced something traumatic or beautiful, I cannot go back to *not* having experienced it.

Yes. You tend to think of this as psychological, which it is. But it is also more than that. It affects the energies of DNA. It affects the blueprint for structures that follow the change. The learning must be experiential for this to happen.

I'm thinking of the channeled writing classes I teach. They are a half day, because people really need to get in a different energy mode in order to begin. It is a kick-start to change. Then people have to follow through on their own in order to make it a lifestyle change. The class is creating an energy memory to work with.

We have been hopeful that more people are interested in this level of personal change. It is not clear to most that it is happening. There is momentum, however.

Being aware of the potentials is a way to see the path ahead. You are on this path. Be free with your willingness to travel. Open to new possibilities in seeing.

I am aware of myself looking down a tunnel to the next opening. I can't see what is beyond it. I only know that I want to go there. Out of curiosity, yes, but also because I am interested in allowing the next layer of energetic growth and learning. The seed has been planted.

The Library Man is smiling. He is humored and encouraged. He throws his hands out, palms up, as if to say 'this is it for now,' and walks away thoughtfully.

To travel and bring energy back from the Spirit World, we must learn how to go there, how to travel into the unknown. This requires that we let go of the Physical World.

It's not that we want to eliminate the Physical World. After all, this is a magnificent gift. It's where we experience dancing and laughing, hugging and loving. What we need to be able to let go of is our intense attachment to it, the holding on that prevents us from moving our attention elsewhere. That is the ego, the me-first part of our psyche that craves attention and control. Focusing our energy there creates an endless cycle of drama and reaction.

The ego is caught up in stories—the stories we use to create our identity, that tell us who we are and who we are not. Everyone's stories have obstacles in them, challenges that we face and do our best to manage. Once the challenges are woven into our story, defining us, they can create restrictions about who we think we are and place limits on what we can be.

We might hear ourselves say, for example: "Things will be alright when ... when I have more money ... when I exercise more ... when the other person changes their behavior ..." Another version of that is: "If only I ... hadn't said that ... if only I *had* said that ... if only my health was better ... if only my mother had loved me." Fill in the blanks in your own story.

There *are* obstacles to living in the physical world. Learning through them is part of being human. If everyone was already perfect, what would be the point of being here? The question is: how much do we let those obstacles limit our choices?

We always have choices. We don't necessarily choose everything that happens to us. There are all kinds of random events every day, many of them are ripples from other people's choices. What we do choose is how we react to what happens to us, how we behave when we have a setback, what we will carry forward with us.

The choices we've made over our lifetime have led us to where we are today. Karma is nothing more than a lap full of consequences, the accumulation of *all* the choices, both skilled and unskilled, that we have made up until now. We can't change what we have chosen in the past. We *can* start choosing something different right now. An important thing we can choose is where to focus our attention.

Universal Wisdom: *You have to be willing to look at your interior life, how you have arranged your beliefs, how you see yourself and others, how you see yourself in relation to yourself and others. You have to be able to look at this and decide if it is in your best interests to function this way.*

It is important to make this examination from a place of stepping back, to look at it objectively. If you are looking at it subjectively, with a lot of emotional attachment to it, then you will get tangled up in the history that made it. Your defense mechanisms will engage. This is a function of the ego, to protect what it sees as its identity, its special place in the world, the things that make it unique.

You have not suffered any more or any less, any deeper, than someone else. Everyone has a story that travels along with their life. Is your ego telling your story, or is it your spirit? The ego has the limited perspective of this lifetime only. Your spirit is connected to multiple dimensions over many lifetimes. It lives in a bigger context. It is not so attached to any one event, certainly not to the ego's story. Do you want your life to be defined by the ego's story, which is fundamentally a soap opera made for daytime tv? Or do you want to be living one glorious chapter in an epic saga stretching over millennia? This is the choice you get to make.

We are talking about stepping into the bigger picture. The story of where you came from and where you are going, traveling the infinite arc of your soul's path. When you step back from the ego, onto this path in the Universe, you will be able to let go of attachment to the outcome of any singular interaction. Travel your soul path. Let your spirit be free of the confines of the ego.

The ego has its purpose. That purpose is to move you through physical existence. Its purpose is not to define the journey or the path. Your journey is the movement of your spirit. The path is the manifestation of Soul.

If our ego is a soap opera and our spirit is a chapter in the Universe, how can we shift our focus from the limited physical world to this larger spiritual context?

I was watching a live-stream of Aretha Franklin's funeral when I heard a very interesting comment. The Reverend Eric Michael Dyson said, "If you aren't already at where you're going, you ain't gonna be there when you arrive." How can I already be there if I haven't gotten there yet? Because Eric Michael Dyson is a Reverend, I think he is probably referring to Heaven. And what is Heaven? Is it really a place up in the clouds with harps and halos? Some external location? I believe that Heaven is *internal*. Heaven is something we create based on our attitudes and actions—our choices. If I want to *get* there, I need to practice *Be*ing there.

'Heaven' just means being fully alive and present in our spiritual life. It's attainable, by practicing the qualities of what it *feels* like to be fully alive and present. Once we recognize the vibration of being alive and present, we can go forward making choices that align with that resonance. We can choose more of it.

༄

Transcendence, Star Travel, the shifting of our perception—these are more than just concepts. They are actions, they are choices that we make that create movement and energetic vibrations. They require that we align ourselves with Universe-energy. To accommodate the higher frequencies of spiritual travel, our inner body needs to be functioning at a high level physically. We also need to slow down our outer activity.

Universal Wisdom: *You are being asked to slow down, not because you need to do less, but because there is another way to move in the world. It occurs at a slower pace.*

You are confused by the idea that your physical energy needs to be elevated, at a vibrational level that matches Spirit, and here you are being asked to slow down. The higher vibrational level is a physical manifestation of Spirit. The slower movement is a way to disconnect from the frenzy of culture. The human world is moving at a pace that precludes spiritual connection.

It is like walking in the forest. You can push yourself through a marathon of times and miles, recording it with technology. Or, you can stop and look at the forest floor, the flowers and insects and clouds and trees. When you are moving quickly it is hard to sync your energy with the natural world.

You understand the benefits of this but you have not yet integrated it into your lifestyle. You are still pushing yourself to do as much as possible every day. Really, you only need to focus on this work, make it the center, and let everything else move into place around it. Set an intention and let it move itself.

This is more than an intention. This is your Soul Path. You have made contact. You know this way of being. Let yourself fall back into the support of it. Be your Original Self, and let the Love of the Universe surround you. Relax, rest in it. Let it feed you.

Join your Spirit on this journey. Let the world go by, the world of human invention and drama. Allow your energy the freedom of Being. In this form, everything will take care of itself. You will have Peace. Release yourself from the chains of the Waking Dream. Enjoy the looping threads of Connected Living.

You know this. Now live it.

Filling our time with doing is not intentional action. It is a habit, possibly an addiction. It is hard to change.
Universal Wisdom: *You have been programmed to believe that nothing will happen unless you plan and push for it. When you behave in this way, then the only things that you will see and take advantage of are those that you have already planned and pushed for. There is an infinite field of opportunities that you cannot even imagine, waiting to join with your intention. Talk about intention.*
I have a note on my desk that says, "Intention is the process of creating future memories." This is a reminder that intention is not about intellectual specifics, but about energetic qualities. The qualities describe resonance, experience, *feelings*, so that I will already have a sensory understanding of the quality when an opportunity comes along which fits that feeling. My qualities list includes these words: joyful gratitude, creative flow, respect, opportunity, harmony.
This is how you will continue. You will allow your mind to do more than your brain, the flow to move through without impedance.
Let the right side do this.
When I try to use the left side of my brain, the side that programs linear function, there is a solid resistance of darkness. When I shift my energy to the right side of my brain, I feel an ease and expansion traveling outside my physical body. I am going to have to learn a new way of thinking, a new way of cranial function.

This is not unlike the re-learning after a stroke or other brain injury. You cannot force the old way to work. You have to redirect the connections. When I let the energy flow through my right brain I feel a pleasant energizing of my whole body, moving in a wave. It is very relaxing. At the same time, the wavelength in my left brain is lengthening. It is making a sound like a sigh. I have been putting too much pressure there.
This is what needs to happen. This will help you to find the sensory qualities of your intention. Practice looking at your life list and feeling the resonance of any of those qualities. You will be better off with less intellectual labeling, more body sensations. It will be the new way.

Our energy is freed by welcoming the unknown, by allowing space. Planning, pushing, and staying busy focuses us in our intellect and compresses our energy. Activities that compress our energy create a stress response as we constantly try to keep up.

In stress response, survival mechanisms drive us to imagine many possible outcomes (all of which have not yet happened and most of which will never happen). Our energy is pushed up into the top of our body, compressed in our heads. We become energetically top-heavy and unbalanced. It is important to re-balance that by consciously moving our energy back into our whole body. This is what is meant by "grounding"—our energy settles and we become more connected to the ground. By freeing our energy, grounding helps us to welcome the unknown with creative space instead of fearing it.

A Teacher arrived to help me with this. She is a woman with cafe au lait skin and a huge billowy afro full of grey hair. She closes her eyes and hums, a resonant sound that moves through her bones.
Oma: *There is a way of being in the world, a way of being that transcends the physical. As you know, transcendence does not mean leaving the physical world. It means incorporating the physical and the spiritual, being both at once. Then you are active in both Point and Zone simultaneously.*

You are going to be entering a new world. You will need to be grounded and undistracted. This is the place to do this.

Oma turns her face skyward and slowly blows air from her O-shaped mouth. Then I do that, too. It brings me back into my lower body. She points a long-nailed finger at me and says *practice that*. I take a deep breath and raise my face to the sky. I shape my mouth into an 'O' and slowly release my breath. I feel my energy move down through my whole body, filling my torso, my legs, my feet, and joining the Earth. I am simultaneously reconnected with the Earth and expanded into the space around me.

Deep exhaling through the 'O' is the kind of breathing that many women instinctively choose during labor to reduce anxiety and connect with their lower bodies. There are many healthy practices that bring peace through this kind of breathing: lap swimming, brisk walking or hiking, yin yoga, meditation, sleeping.[18] These practices produce extended, even, in-and-out breaths. Rhythmic. Creating energy balance through release and revitalization.

Oma points up to the sky. I look up and see the clouds, fluffy and flowing, like her hair. She smiles and winks at me. She tucks her head and curls her back, forming her body into a ball and becoming a cloud. Her hand appears out of the side of the cloud-ball and waves good bye to me.

See you, then. See you Everywhere.
I hear her lips smack a little goodbye kiss. I feel pleasantly happy and relaxed.

༄

We can look to Nature to show us how to let go. In Northern Minnesota, fall is spectacular. We often say, "The trees are about to show us how lovely it is to let go." The deciduous plants change into a wardrobe of neon color, and when the winter wind comes and combs the Earth's hair, it all falls away. The trees have to let go

---

[18] Interestingly, this is also the kind of breathing that smokers practice many times every day, although it is paired with a harmful drug.

of their leaves in order to make room for the next season, where they will rest in their roots and replenish themselves, readying for the return of spring. Like the trees, we have many opportunities to understand the benefits of making space. We have to let go of one thing for the next thing to happen.

I experienced this when I had to let go of something very dear to me: my upright piano. It had become clear that there was not enough room in my tiny one-room home to justify keeping such a large instrument, especially when I had little time to play it. Still, I struggled with the change. I had so much attachment to its history in my life. Its wooden-bodied emotional resonance had supported me through many difficult times. It was part of my identity. When I gave away my piano and it left, I wept.

Once the piano was gone, however, my living space changed in an amazing way. There was so much more room! Whole windows were unblocked and my view expanded. I exchanged my couch for a sofa bed and now, because there was room to open the bed, my children and friends could visit overnight. A wise friend offered me a small, portable instrument—a ukulele. Then I unexpectedly came across an old saxophone in a storage closet. There was other music to be made! The benefits of change just kept piling up.

The most surprising shift came when I rearranged the furniture. Some stuff just didn't fit right, some things had to go away and other things came in. I added a cabinet that had a good top for my plants. I had no idea what would go in that cabinet but held space for whatever that needed to be. It turned out to be the perfect place for an altar. In all my moving around I hadn't had an altar for several years.

An altar is very personal. On it I place objects, words, pictures, candles, herbs—things that help me stay focused on my healing and my purpose. The items vary over time, just like my process. I spend some time each day seated before the altar meditating. I keep the doors open when I'm home alone. I close the doors when I have guests, to keep the energy clean and unscrutinized by others' curiosity.

So much enrichment entered my life, all because I was willing to give up the known for the unknown. I made room. I held space and allowed the Universe to move me.

There is a Buddhist concept called 'storehouse consciousness.' It describes the idea that everything we do is either the fruit of a seed planted in the past or a seed we are planting now for the future. When we repeat our old behavior patterns, we are just planting the same seeds over and over. This means that we will continue to reap the same fruit over and over in the future. If I can interrupt my behavior and choose other seeds to plant for the future, I will reap a different fruit when those seeds mature.

If I want to move into greater consciousness, I will need to stop planting the behavior seeds that tether me to five sense reality. I will need to start planting the behavior seeds that expand my perception beyond the five senses. I will need to tend that garden.

Since the garden we are tending is the Unknown, one of the seeds we will need to plant will be Trust. We cannot pin down the Unknown, because it is by its nature *unknown*.

> "...There is a tremendous sense of exhilaration if we can take the jump and move into the unknown, even if the idea scares us to death. And when we take trust to the level of the quantum leap, we don't make any elaborate plans or preparations. We don't say, "Okay, I trust that I know what to do now, and I'll settle my things and pack my suitcase and take it with me." No, we just jump, with hardly a thought of what happens next."
> ~ Osho[19]

In order to move into the Unknown, we need to be able to let go of knowing, the desire to pin down facts and outcomes. I once dreamed that I was in a foreign city, a huge city somewhere in Asia.

---

[19] *Osho Zen Tarot* (St. Martin's Press, 1994), p. 60.

I had gone into a building with my two good friends. We came out and somehow turned in opposite directions. I had not gone more than a few steps when I realized they weren't with me, and quickly turned around. I backtracked, thinking about the travelers' rule: don't wander around, always go back to the place you last saw each other. But of course we had not discussed this ahead of time and I didn't think they knew about it. So I went the way they had gone.

I stepped out into the street where I could see the people on the sidewalk as I passed them. I checked out every person's face one by one, but when I came to the end of the block I still had not seen them. We had no phones, no way to communicate. I knew where we were supposedly heading, I had a picture of it in my mind, and I turned that direction. When I turned, the scene suddenly changed. Nothing looked familiar. The streets were crammed with moving people and cars. I had no idea where I was. I was lost.

I woke up from this dream with a feeling that is all too familiar to me after brain injury—complete disorientation. It occurs regularly in my daily life, even in my very small town, even in my own home. It is the sensation of being unmoored from reality. Sometimes, when I am very tired, I feel momentary panic or despair. When it is prolonged, I might start to cry. It is a feeling of being so vulnerable that even my ego is useless. I have learned, however, to breathe and relax into it, to let the moment be as it is. I have learned to let go of my need to be oriented and in control.

Once I relax, I expand into space and allow the arrival of creative energy. It always shows up. I don't know what or when, but I trust that it will. Then a way forward appears. It's rarely the way I would have normally have coped, since I can't even conjure a memory of what that would've been. The way forward is usually something new and interesting. It's often humorous and I laugh out loud. I have come to know that it's not important to do things the same way twice (even basic tasks like cooking or dressing). Often, the new way seems much more helpful and interesting.

I woke up from my dream of being lost with not only the familiar feeling of disorientation, but also with the awareness that this was an important place to be in life. It's not a mistake. This disorientation is giving me many opportunities to practice Not Knowing. Expectation of a known or predictable outcome holds me down to a very small Point, where energy movement is restricted. Stepping off the path of expectation opens me up to Space, where energy expands and creativity is allowed. This is the way into the Great Mystery, into transcendence, into the Void. It is outside of me. It is within me. It is the joining of every thing and every not-thing. It feels beautiful.

I was reminded of this during another time of struggle. I was signing legal financial papers after my father's death and I had no idea what I was doing. I'd never needed to deal with this kind of thing before. I began to panic. I didn't know who to trust.
Universal Wisdom: *Why do you have to trust anybody?*
Because this is likely my last shot, the last chance on my horizon, to have this kind of opportunity. I don't know what lies ahead.
Haven't we been taking care of you?
Yes, yes, and yes. I have ended up everywhere I need to be. I am standing at the doorway to another opening in my life, without parents or children to care for, with the book series moving on its way.
  Hmmm. I can see how lack of Trust, how fear and anxiety, are holding me back. By placing my attention there, I am not freeing myself to move forward or entertain positive thoughts and intentions.
You don't have to make any decision this very minute. Nothing has actually happened yet. You have just signed some papers. Carry on as if the world is holding you in its arms. Walk the path which your ancestors have made for you. This contribution is one of the steps on that path.
I have been all tangled up in trying to create some kind of security, for myself and for my children in the future. I might as well say it out loud: I am afraid for my children and their children. The planet is rebalancing and human structures are going to collapse.
That is what it takes to create something new. Weren't you just reading

last night about disruptive thinking?[20]

It's good for me to be aware of this. After cancer I felt that I had no energy for Joy and have been reorganizing my life to regain that. Now I realize that I am letting fear co-opt my Trust. Ah, yes—recreating Joy and Trust brings me Home. Centered in my own seed, celebrating Life, trusting the path of my ancestors, this is my Home. It is the place I have been missing. It is the place I want to be.

It is the place you belong.

Thank you so much. I have refocused my attention.

There will always be things to draw your attention away from Home, but the more you live in your Home, the easier it will be to return. Do not put too much concern into the times you are off the path. It is just the way life is, to be distracted and then come Home again and again.

Like my current focus on tasks that don't feed me—don't invest so much energy there, just get it done and move on.

It is one of the lessons related to limited energy resources, which everyone has to some extent. Some things cannot take your time and energy at all. Some things have to be attended to but with limited time and energy. Other things need your direct and sustained attention. Moving The Gift is your primary purpose in life. Everything else needs to be ordered around that.

Suddenly everything seems more beautiful, more manageable, more focused. I am a human vehicle that moves the gift.

And it is a beautiful journey when you are aware and present.

Joy and Trust.

Exactly.

Big Thanks always.

We are with you. See us. Rely on us. Honor us.

Joy. Trust. Home.

Go In Peace.

---

[20] *Traveling Light*, chapter 4.

~ 3 ~

Vibrational Healing

Our first experience of transcendence often occurs in a spiritual environment: immersed in Nature, during meditation, within a house of worship, or creating art. These can be illuminating and life-changing experiences on a personal level. They are, however, just starting points. Our greater task is to bring the practice of transcendence into our daily lives and to infuse our living with these vibrations.

One of the most difficult places to apply this is in personal relationships. Human relationships are built on interactions of the ego—they are expressions of the dynamic between our own ego and that of others. Ego has the important function of protecting us, of defending us from harms in the past, present and future. When we become entangled in these emotional reactions, however, we are limiting our ability to expand into the vibration of transcendence.

Everything we experience as humans is a vibration translated by our body into a sensation. Our eyes record the vibration of light. Our ears take in sound waves. Our skin responds to the nerve pulses of pressure. The situations that produce all of these energies are present in the world whether we take them in or not. It is our body that experiences and translates them. Emotions are sensations too—they are translated vibrations.

> "An emotion is like a sound: it's an internal interpretation of an external vibration. The vibration is not the feeling. Feelings don't exist around us. They are made inside us and can be remade there, too."
> ~Holiday Mathis

With awareness, we can choose how we translate vibrations and how we respond. We can shift our attention from the limited personal focus of emotional reaction toward the broader energy existing in collective Space. We can shift toward vibrational healing.

A'riquea: *Feelings are chemical reactions in your body. Chemical reactions are energy reactions. They are read by sensors in the body. They can be signposts. The energy sensors will alert you to a direction that needs to be taken, whether you want to go towards or away from a given energy stimulus. Of course, there is always the choice not to move in any direction, and just note the sensations.*

These sensations are important in the process of survival and evolution. They inform a Being of the quality of a stimulus. The reaction to it can save a life, enhance a life, improve evolution. A problem today is that humans are constantly bombarded with feelings, actually encouraged to amass more and more feelings. Think about plants and animals. Their stimuli vary, but the intensity of that variation is only occasionally worth reacting to. Humans have come to believe that everything requires a reaction. Then the reactions create more reactions which create more reactions. The human system is overwhelmed.

When I consider the energy patterns and habits of my childhood, I see how things became so muddy and unrecognizable that I learned to assume everything was a threat. It's taken most of my life to untangle that.

It is the human condition. And that has been layered onto with the explosion in technology and the sheer numbers of humans interacting on the planet. Even if you are not directly interacting, that energy is still there. This is why meditation is so important—it brings you away from the interactive field and into communication with your own body, mind, and spirit. It is a stepping back. Reaction is not necessary. Rest and repair are.

Reactions aren't necessary, but they often follow patterns—well-worn energy habits that are difficult to dissolve. I can't just say "I don't want to do this anymore," and Poof! it disappears. The channels created by my past experiences are deep grooves. Emotions are like water, and they naturally run into those deep grooves. It's a lot of work to fill in the grooves or create new ones to divert the flow. Sometimes the pace feels glacial. But what is the alternative? To keep doing the same unhelpful things and hope for a different outcome? Over time, shifting my behavior and changing my patterns improves my quality of life. Sometimes, just creating awareness can be life-changing. Here's an example:

I built the one-room studio where I live with my own two hands. Electricity was not available in my rural area at the time, but I put wiring in the walls just in case. Over a decade later, electricity arrived. I hooked up all my outlets. Finances kept me from purchasing light fixtures. The electrician told me that because I had "hot" wires (unattached to fixtures), he could not connect everything to the fuse box. For the entire first year I had power on only one side of my house. In order to turn on a light or use the printer I ran maze of of extension cords around the perimeter of the walls, from the light side to the dark side.

One night, I had a gathering at my house. I had to leave early and told people to just turn off the lights and close the door when they left. I came home much later that night to find the yard light on—the yard light that had not worked once since the house was electrified because it's on the side of the house with no power. I was stunned. How could this have occurred??

I went in the house and tried the switch. On. Off. On. Off. It worked. I went all around the house plugging things into outlets on the "dark" side of the house. They *all* worked. Unbelievable. I had never even tried them. Not once. For an entire year, I believed that the sockets did not work, just because someone told me they wouldn't. I laughed out loud! And, I felt like a dang fool.

It made me wonder how many *other* things I was going along with in my life just because it was what I'd been told. I'm not pretty, because my mother told me that? I'm too intense, because someone else doesn't want to deal with emotional intimacy? Being a channeler makes me weird, just because other people don't understand it? Wow. Such a simple thing as flipping a light switch led me to see how I could improve whole areas of my life just by illuminating the problem or looking at the wiring—by challenging my beliefs.

Like the electrical issue in my home, unhealed patterns create circuits of belief and behavior that limit the full expression of our spirituality. They form energy clots and encourage us to maintain wasteful workarounds. We can see these blockages at work in our ego's reaction to the relationships around us.

While I cared for my father during his year in hospice, the pitfalls in our relationship came into sharper focus. He had been uncomfortable with deep emotional conversation his whole life. Then, exploring feelings with him became even more difficult as he detached from the physical plane. Ultimately, I was not able to repair our broken relationship. I did, however, have many opportunities to look at my own emotional functioning. I was able to examine the sense of obligation and resentment that came with providing his care.

A'riquea: *It's always the same, isn't it? You want something out of a relationship and then you are disappointed to find it's not there. You cannot change the relationship, you can only change your expectations of it. Would you allow any other person to take up so much space in your daily life without some kind of mutual sharing?*

We have talked about this before. It's not what you see, it's how you see it. Your father has his own learning trajectory in life. And so do you. How they line up defines how you will feel about your interactions. During hospice I became aware of my dad's deep sense of abandonment. He had often talked during his life about the circumstances, but not the feelings attached to them. His own father, and then his mother, died when he was very young. He was out in the world alone. His wife became his only family. Growing up, I often felt emotionally abandoned by both my parents. They did what they were capable of but their lack of emotional skills created a lot of damage. Within these life circumstances, I wondered what it meant to be there for someone through thick and thin. Hospice with my father was one of the thinner times.

You are inserting a lot of psycho-babble into this situation. It may be true, but it does not resolve the tension you feel. It may explain it, but it doesn't address it.

What do you suggest?

That you work on your own self, your own energy arrangement. Do not follow the pattern just because it is expected. Bring something new into where you place your energy. You are thinking, of course, about how you arrange your energy with him. But in order to change, you will need to look at how you arrange your energy with yourself. This is the intention from which all things manifest.

My relationship with myself.

Your relationship with your energy.

When I hear that and stop to feel my energy, I sense the expansiveness of Zone and feel better in that space. When I embody my relationship with my father, my energy moves up out of my legs and pelvis, into my head, and extends toward him. My vital energy is draining outward to accommodate him and I am off-balance, out of my spiritual center. It mirrors the only way he felt comfortable relating to me as I grew up. He must feel that way now when we are interacting, whether he is aware of it or not.

When I practice metta energy—loving kindness for myself and others, I am relaxed and enriched and fully in myself. This is how I want to be approaching everything in my life, including my interactions with my dying father. A Teacher told me recently: your energy must be high, but your activity must slow or cease—your physical activity, but also ego activity.

Try to practice this when you speak with him, see what happens.

Thank you so much. I need to be taking care of my own business, first and foremost.

If your house is not in order, your relationships will reflect that imbalance. Although it was a bit of a journey to get there, I was eventually able to step out of ego function and focus less on what was missing in our relationship. I was able to move my attention into the broader context of The All where we both existed. There, I came to the awareness that gratefully assuming responsibility for my elder provided a gift for us both.

Everybody's ability to acknowledge, honor and create their own energy is in constant flux. It's tested over and over as we come into contact with the dynamics of other people's energy. Considering all of the egos careening around and bumping into each other, I know that *I* am the only one who is in charge of my own situation. I also see that those energy dynamics create opportunities for learning, with the energy of this learning going back to The One.

A'riquea: *This is a good thing to be thinking about, because the current social and political climate in your culture has become confrontational. The collision of egos is affecting the overall energy of human existence. You want to be thinking about your own energy, because that is really the only place where you can actually be effective. It is difficult to separate the ego energy from spiritual energy because, as you know, they occupy the same space. But it is important to be able to pull back enough from the perspective of Ego to be able to connect with Spirit. This lines up with the directive to embody a spirit-led life. This was discussed at length in the first book, so we are not going to go into that in depth here.*

In all of these situations involving boundaries, you will have a better outcome when you are able to recognize your Spirit, when you are able to choose movement that feeds Spirit, and to carry that through. It is a learning process, there will be errors along the way. But overall, the more you practice, the more you will be able to sense the difference, and the more you will be able to function from this position.

As was discussed in the second book, this is about choosing where you place your attention. It is not something that is done occasionally. It is a way of Being. It takes practice. The more you practice, the more comfortable you will be in this energy arrangement, and the more you will function like this in your everyday life.

You will want to be doing this, because you will see how it improves your own life. It also improves the path that humans are evolving along.

Go ahead and write down what you are thinking.

Sometimes when I set my own boundaries I worry about hurting the other person involved. Your words help me realize that this is not a problem if I am coming from a place of spiritual clarity. All it requires is placing my attention on the energy coordinates of Spirit, rather than Ego. The ego is compact energy, limited to the immediate Point of my physical body and its reactions. Within that same space is the expanded dimension of Spirit, which includes the energy-space both inside and also outside my body. Ego energy is like being tightly screwed down to the floor. Spirit energy is like being a bird released into the sky.

I recently experienced two situations that showed the two sides of the ego coin. In the first, a man was pursuing me. He was continually pushing his physical energy into my space even after I asked him to back off. It felt like he was a predator and I was his prey. I felt unsafe even at home. I was being stalked. I chose to defend myself by turning my self inward and becoming invisible. In the second situation, I felt an obligation to provide home medical care for an extended period of time, even though it was draining my energy. I was unable to control the outward dissipation and internal emptiness which that created. Both of these situations—disappearing inward and outward—demonstrate unbalanced ego positions.

It's interesting to note that just in describing those situations, I feel my energy getting pulled back into ego function. I feel myself losing the spaciousness of Spirit. When I talk about the spaciousness, I come back to it. So moving back and forth between Ego and Spirit is that simple. How do I maintain spiritual space when my ego is confronted in either of these situations? I hear the answer: it's where I place my attention. Maintaining spiritual space is a matter of practice. Then I heard these words, too: Firm, Clear, Consistent. That sounds a lot like parenting.

It is very much like parenting. What you are trying to do is provide support and guidance for your own self. Berating yourself for errors, focusing on the problem, or ignoring the situation will not be helpful. Focusing on solutions, creating opportunities, and acknowledging success will have better outcomes.

It's important to think about this not from the small perspective of the ego, that somehow this behavior is going to make all of your relationships magically heal. What it is meant to do is to enrich the space that you function in and also the energy of related dimensions. This is an evolutionary directive that has positive personal benefits. Don't try to solve an ego problem using the ego. Solve an ego problem with spiritual energy, and know that you are also becoming part of dimensional evolution. Become One With All.

⁂

It is important to be aware of our own vibrations and actively choose how we want to express them. As one of my Sufi friends says, "Don't do harm, do Harmony." There are many ways that relationships are either harmed or harmonized. We can say, for example, that honesty is an important part of healthy relationships. But dishonesty is not one thing—it occurs along a continuum with varying effects.

Dishonesty is about making something seem like something it is not. Everyone is dishonest sometimes. People can be dishonest by wearing social masks—by showing the world who they would like to be rather than who they are. If my main mode of operation is to deny my true self, then I am also being dishonest with myself.

Dishonesty turns into actual lying when someone *knows* they are not telling the truth. Being dishonest with my friend to prevent her from finding out about her surprise party is intentional lying, but it's not harmful. Other lies are emotionally deeper and more damaging. Some are deliberately covered up. Betrayal is, essentially, living a lie—protecting one's own ego to avoid owning the harm created for another.

I can't control other people's choices around honesty, but I can control mine. A friend and I planned an activity together. When I checked in with her on the day we were going, I found that she had changed the time and had also invited another person. She had not included me in any of those decisions or even informed me of the change. I had another commitment at the new time and wasn't able to go. She brushed off my surprise and frustration as unimportant. She wasn't willing to acknowledge the harm created by her dishonesty.

Initially, I was angry. But then I realized that I had a choice in how I would react. I explored three voices—Ego, Spirit, and Soul—in response to the situation, and here's what they each had to say:

Ego, reacting to the hurt: *You Bitch!*

Spirit, seeing the bigger picture: *Your friend has made some mistakes. She did not intend to harm you. There has been a lack of communication here.*

Soul, allowing Space: *Now you're free to go out in the woods by yourself and harvest some chaga today for tea.*

So, who would I listen to? What actions would follow that choice? I made the tea.

Dishonesty is a problem because it erodes trust. If I am lying about one thing, how would you know if I was telling the truth about something else? Lying destabilizes the foundation of trust in our relationship. Rebuilding a relationship damaged by lying takes ownership. Being angry about getting caught or denying the lie is, of course, defensive behavior. Owning it, like any difficult behavior, means that I admit and apologize for doing it. Maybe I lied to stay out of trouble, or to protect my own pride. Maybe I just changed my mind and didn't tell you. Or I forgot. Apologizing for my behavior means that I don't push the blame on something or someone else. I say I'm sorry, not just for lying, but for harming our relationship.

And I practice patience while you learn to trust me again.

For the most part, people don't intend to hurt each other. But lack of intention alone does not erase the harm done. In basketball, fouls are called when a player does something that is against the rules—usually something that endangers the safety of other players. The foul is based on the *action*, not on the intention. Intention is something that may vary depending on who is describing it, making it hard to prove. An action is visible. The ref calls a foul, a penalty is given which benefits the team that was fouled, and everyone moves on. Players who commit enough fouls are removed from the game. If there were no consequences for their actions, no one would care if they committed a foul. The game would become physically brutal and people would be injured. The player or team that is wronged receives reparations in the form of free shots at the basket.

In her book *The Storyteller*, Jodi Picoult explores harm and forgiveness through the much more serious context of holocaust survivors: "To be forgiven, the person has to be sorry. In Judaism, it's called *teshuvah*. It means 'turning away from evil.' It's not a one-time deal, either. It's a course of action. A single act of repentance is something that makes the person who committed the evil feel better, but not the person against whom the evil was committed…. You don't make peace only with God. You make it with people. Sin isn't global. It's personal. If you do wrong to someone, the only way to fix that is to go to that same person and do right by them." [21] And do right *by them*. Which means acknowledging the harm committed and not turning away from it.

In our culture, the word apology is often used as a substitute for the word atonement, but they are not the same thing. The dictionary makes this clear. The definition of *apology* is: a regretful acknowledgment of an offense or failure. The word comes from the Greek *apologia*, 'a speech in one's own defense.' The definition of *atonement*, on the other hand, is: reparation for a wrong or injury. Its definition is influenced by the medieval Latin *adunamentum*,

---

[21] Pocket Books (2013), p. 202.

which means unity, or 'making one.'

In other words, an apology is a speech in one's own defense, while atonement is an action that repairs a broken connection. Apologizing, even apologizing profusely, has a limited effect if its main purpose is to address or relieve the perpetrator's guilt. True atonement reaches out to the other person's heart and offers healing on their terms. It takes the one who has been dishonest out of their own ego and brings healing into shared energy space with the one harmed.

I have a spiritual responsibility to take ownership of my hurtful actions by healing the vibrations created. That heals me, heals my relationships, and replaces negative energy with positive in the energy space of the Universe.

There are situations where neither apology nor atonement can occur. Sometimes the one who has created harm is not willing, able, or available to make reparations. Healing is still possible. In *Grandmother Dreams*, The Teachers discuss this broken connection and its healing.

Universal Wisdom: *It is possible to fully heal without the input of the other doing the harm. It is a longer path. The one who has harmed another will always have the responsibility to heal that which they have created, but healing in the one hurt is not dependent on that. The harm itself creates a disruption to the Movement of Spirit. That is what is so distressing to the one harmed. What is most important to healing is the re-creation of the environment that allows Movement of Spirit.*[22]

I would like to think that I can create spiritual space with anyone, that I can forgive any level of behavior. In a Universal context, this is true. I can easily see how we are all influenced by our family, our culture, our experiences, and our skill level in the moment. We are all learning. On a personal level, I am on the longer path. I am still learning how to choose relationships that nurture me, that are

---

[22] *Grandmother Dreams*, p. 61-62.

mutual and honest and caring. I am learning to disengage from those that are not. I am learning to honor my spiritual space, to nurture my spiritual vibrations.

> "Everyone goin' ta hurt ya, you decide
> which ones goin' ta make ya suffer."
> ~ Bob Marley

☙

While I am learning to nurture my spiritual vibration, I have the opportunity to observe my reactions. Reacting often follows a personal pattern, something learned through regular repetition. Continuing to react to others' behavior in the same way over and over is like running on a mouse-wheel of ego function.

One of my patterns is related to being an empath, to being very sensitive to the energy of others. This is not a bad thing, but it is something I need to be aware of and manage. I am porous and easily triggered. I have to set energy boundaries to keep myself sane and functioning. It is difficult for me to interact with friends who have lower empathy, because they appear to be rejecting or using me.

Other people cannot help who they are any more than I can help who I am. I often expect them to be more sensitive or responsive, and they are not. I can love them for who they are but I can't rely on them to meet my needs for compassion and personal enfolding. Then I have to set a boundary around how much I interact with them and what my expectations of those interactions will be. I want to be less reactive.

Universal Wisdom: *This is something you have struggled with your whole life.*

Ironic, isn't it, that I am so aware of other peoples' feelings but have been unable to see that they are not the same as mine?

This perspective is something that everyone works on during their lifetime. The best relationships recognize that the other person is someone different, with their own history and way of functioning in the world. You will be happier when you let expectations of sameness fall away.

This is not to say that you do not hold people accountable. It is important to let people know when they have overstepped a boundary and hurt you. It is not your responsibility to create the consequence, only to state your perspective. People often need to hear the same thing from multiple people over time before they really believe that something applies to them and is worth addressing.

What is it that I am missing about my own behavior?

You have a hard time seeing how taking things personally is actually a selfish behavior. It takes the other person's behavior and makes it your problem, when it is not. Their behavior may make for a difficult friendship dynamic, but it is not about you.

You can move away from this way of reacting by focusing your attention on your reaction. Not on what caused *the reaction, but how you have taken in the information and processed it as a negative. That is about you, not the other person.*

It's tempting to go to the bigger context, to "just" get out of ego reaction and consider Spirit.

This is a good practice, but not always useful. It is worthwhile to observe your reaction, because this will inform you of your habits and energy patterns. It is not so much that you must examine them under a microscope and parse out every psychological cause. That is a rabbit hole with no end to it. What you want to be able to do is recognize when you are having a patterned, or learned, reaction and then *move your energy to create a new pattern. This is about balance. Not buying into the reaction, of course, but also not giving it too much attention and energy.*

When we are unaware of our patterns, we may react by taking our own problem and making it someone else's. We may also react taking someone else's problem and making it ours. As a culturally well-trained female, for example, I used to be a need-filling machine. I took on everyone else's problems and always said Yes to anything asked of me. Living with chemo fatigue, however, I had to learn to say No to many things. I had to learn to prioritize how I was going to use my limited energy resources.

The process of learning to say No showed me how I regularly set myself up for "rescue" behaviors. It's a role I played. I have called it Making A Difference over the years, as if that puts it on a higher spiritual plane. But how much of it was actually about feeding my ego—how I needed to see myself in the world to justify my existence? I started calling it Hero Status.

The Hero is one point in a triangle of roles that work together—the Victim, the Perpetrator, and the Hero. No one wants to be a victim, and it is also distasteful to think of oneself as a perpetrator. That leaves the Hero, the one who is going to save the day and rescue the victim from the perp.

Of course, the roles are not so separate. No one is just one of those things. I wish I'd never done anything bad to someone else, or myself, but I have. And I will in the future, even though I wish that wasn't true. I don't want to feel like a victim, but there will always be the bad choices of other people to deal with. If I set myself up as a hero, I fool myself into believing I don't have to be the other two things. But being the hero helps to create and perpetuate the triangle. It shoves other people into the two roles that I have rejected. The solution is to realize that everybody is all three of those things, and more, and to realize that even the triangle itself exists in an even larger context.

Pretending that I can be the Hero *only* is patterned ego behavior. Patterns sometimes feel safe because they are familiar. Stepping away from them does not have to feel dangerous. As I change, I can still address and meet my needs as long as I am focusing on my *spiritual* needs.

An example of this was the shift needed for me to cope after my double mastectomy. I had recurring dreams of my breasts, excised and sitting in a formalin jar or freezer somewhere, detached parts of my body that I was lonely for and that might be lonely for me. To let them go, I created a ritual that thanked them for taking the cancer with them when they left, thanking them for being something so easily removable (unlike my brain or lungs). This ceremony loosened my attachment.

There was a related adjustment that was much more difficult to make. In Western society women are defined by their breasts. My sexuality had to be reconsidered and reconfigured. Although this was a lengthy process, I ended up thanking cancer for the opportunity to go into my future without the burden of a culturally-defined sexuality. I was able to let go of the need for external validation of my physical presence. I re-owned my body with a full chest tattoo of spiritual significance. All of it involved a lot of internal processing around patterns and attachment. The most difficult part was incorporating it all into an intimate relationship with another person.

A'riquea: *You have done a good job of thinking this through. Of course, it will not be so easy to put it into practice. It helps to have seen the patterns. Roles are more difficult to change because they involve other people. Interacting with others who expect the usual pattern will draw you back into performing a role. There is safety in the role. It is like a dance, where everyone knows the steps. When you choose to step out, people's reactions will tempt you to get back in line.*

There are applications to Point and Zone here. The usual patterns require linear behavior—one thing follows another in a predictable way. Stepping out means moving into Space, where all things are possible. Playing a role is the same as getting stuck in a Point, getting stuck in one way of doing things, without honoring the creative process. When you step out, you will be playing with creativity. There will be complaints, and even backlash.

There are different ways to look at this. Creativity for creativity's sake, art for art's sake, is its own box of attachment. It is not unlike following the rules just to follow the rules. Both are thoughtless and heartless. Your challenge will be knowing what your needs are and making choices to feed yourself. Of course, we are not talking about Ego's needs, which describe attachment. We are talking about Spirit's needs.

And what are Spirit's needs? Moving energy, moving energy between Points, through the Zone. Moving energy between people.

Moving Love energy, which is compassion and joy. We have talked of this before. Living involves sensation, being aware of sensation in the body, being aware of vibration in the body, and moving it in Space. You must understand your energy relationship to Point and to Zone, and work with both of them.

Learning to change patterned behavior is a process. We try to address our behavior by doing something different.
Universal Wisdom: *This is what either forges relationships together or forces them apart. Each person is an individual with their own path through the world. When the paths join it is because there are similarities. You have the opportunity to practice doing things a different way. Be very clear on this—it is a choice.*

The choice is to fall back on old patterns and repeat them, or to see the patterns and choose to try something else. The Something Else is a trial. Hopefully, you will be able to tell what works and what doesn't. The way to tell is the vibration. The vibration in your body. It is possible to feel safe and secure because you are given freedom and control. It is also possible to feel this way because you are shut down. One feels like an opening, the other like a closing. If you are turning away, you are closing down. If you are turning toward, you are opening.

Life is complex. What works in one situation may not work in another. Healing trauma is a long path of trial and error. Everyone has some trauma. It is part of living. What you do with the trauma determines which way you will grow. Remember the discussion of the blueprint, with the matrix built on that framework.[23] Trauma can be part of the blueprint and it can be part of the matrix. The beauty of Life is the vibration that occurs within the framework of the matrix. It is not the matrix itself, although that is necessarily part of it. But it has more

---

[23] Blueprint and matrix are discussed in detail in *Traveling Light*, p. 28-44. Basically, the blueprint is a foundation encoded by DNA, and the matrix is all of the experiences—physical, emotional and spiritual—that create an energy presence connected to that blueprint. It is a constant work in progress.

to do with the vibration created by the existence of the matrix, and that vibration is generated by the Soul within. Shining a light on the Soul Path creates an energy that allows the matrix to vibrate, to resonate at a clearer frequency. The spirit-fed life illuminates the Soul Path, increases its brilliance. It burns away the barbs, the sticking points, that reduce flow and freedom. It allows more Being.

We want you to know that we are here for you, we are supporting this kind of growth and change. Enter into healing with the support of the Universe. It is in everyone's best interest. That you see your pain and injury in the light of growth and healing, that you continue to move, that you continue to expand, and that you fill the space created with the energy of Love and Light. This is your purpose. It is why you are here.

As we heal, the Doing-Something-Different doesn't always go as planned. Mistakes are made. If we are open, these become opportunities for learning.

I had a long-standing friendship which seemed to sour over time. Whenever we got together I felt judged and pushed away. Hurtful situations were created. This was difficult for me because I valued our spiritual connection. For a long time I tried to just brush it off. Finally, I could not go on without addressing these behaviors and we had a meeting where I expressed my concerns.

Overall, I thought it was a good interaction. I took the opportunity to examine my own patterns, set some boundaries, and address the conflict mindfully. I was able to do this with a reasonable person. We did not come out of it being all lovey-dovey, healed into a perfect world. But a crack of light entered into a dark place and seeds were planted. Afterward, I received feedback from my Teachers about it.

A'riquea: *This is an interesting situation. Some of the hurt has been manufactured by you and the responsibility placed on another person. It's not that these past interactions didn't occur. Obviously they did. What you understood to be happening then was colored by your filters.*

It's not that your experience was false, it's that you took away from it what you needed to keep your story going—that your friend has abandoned you. Your friend has moved a great distance away from the arrangement that started your relationship, that is true. You have gone on with your life as best you could, especially in the face of major illness.

It was important for the two of you to reconnect. It is something that we need to have happen. I'm not sure that this is what we had in mind, this action, but it has started you on a better path. This is desirable.

I have to admit that I am feeling a little hurt by this information. I made a problem out of nothing? Is that just my patterns talking again, feeling disgraced at honoring my feelings?

Well, it could be. It is not helpful to get too tangled up in the emotions of this situation, or any situation. What is important is to be able to pull away and step into the larger picture, the spirit-fed perspective. That is why the details of what occurred here are not so important. It is the energy of the outcome that is of interest.

As I said earlier, I did not feel that we came to a higher vibration, not immediately anyway. My ego was hoping for greater resolution, and it was only partial. I do feel better about reconnecting with the spiritual foundation of our relationship. That has always been the bottom line, the thing I did not want to discard. Maybe I took a round about way to get there?

Round about, maybe. You have also inserted some reality into the other person's life. We're not sure it was your place to do that, but now there it is.

And here's my ego, jumping in to feel ashamed that I took an action that was not Right. Here I thought I had been so mindful and respectful. What would have been a better way to do this or a different thing to do?

You could have realized your patterns and decided to create your boundary and point out hurtful behavior in the future, without making this into a bigger conflict.

I am feeling defensive here.

You are feeling the energy history of having your feelings discounted. This is the pattern that brought you to take the action with your friend.

This is the pattern that is evidencing in our interaction right now. It is a pattern that you also visit upon yourself, discounting your feelings.

You need not be so hard on yourself for any mistakes you have made. You do need to learn how to pull back and allow your feeling to be just part of the flow of Universe.

It's possible to spend a lot of energy trying to fix problems with others that actually belong to me. These problems are ego attachments to familiar vibrations. On-going ego attachments are evidence of stored negativity.

I held on to the pain of my divorce for a very long time, like it was some kind of prize. As if life isn't hard enough without collecting pain trophies! I wondered why I would choose that—was I was doing that for other people to see, or for me to prove something to myself?

Universal Wisdom: *You are building a world with it. You think that it proves you are alive. Pain is a feeling. When you deny yourself in the physical world, you are not able to accept the gifts that Life gives you. Collecting negativity is a back-door way of being in the world. It allows you an escape. When gifts are offered, when the chance to feel alive is offered, then you go back to these "trophies." You use this pain to say "Look, I already have feelings, I don't need more."*

You use pain as a shield, to keep you from having to look at Life in a positive way. You develop a relationship with the pain to avoid a relationship with Love. You use the pain to explain why you cannot receive Love—because you are broken, because you are damaged, because you're not ready, because you don't deserve it. Pain is a habit. It is an addiction just like everything else.

Sometimes when I am with positive people, I find myself judging them as being pollyanna, as being not real, as if they have not experienced Life because they haven't had enough pain to know what "real" life is like. Real life hurts you. Real life prunes you like a bonsai tree. Of course, everyone has pain. Some people are better at denying it, or hiding it or avoiding it. I am wearing it like a banner. Look at me, I am alive, I am more real. Sometimes when I see someone who is homeless or drug-addicted and suffering a great deal, I criticize myself for not being as real as they are.

It's also true that some are more sensitive to pain. Pain is a feeling. There are all kinds of feelings. You can choose which kind of feelings you prefer to have. That will make your journey lighter or heavier. And it is not "having" the feelings that is your earthly experience, it is the movement of feelings. This is back to the movement of Love, which is compassion. Holding pain creates a block to any kind of movement. Moving pain creates a flow for all kinds of feelings.

For anything to be a feeling, it has to have some physical effect in the body—we feel feelings with our body. It is an energy movement. *And it is generated by the movement of energy between Points. As we have discussed, the Points are not in a static arrangement. There is constant flow in and out of them. This flow, through Space, in the Zone, is what creates a feeling in the body. As the energy moves, it has contact with other Points.*

Pain is a feeling, a movement of energy, that encourages Points to close down. There is a defensive reaction. Holding pain hardens the points against energy flow. Non-elastic Points cause stagnation in the Zone. Good health requires energetic vibration in the Zone. This is something you need, energetic vibration in the Zone, the Zone around every Point in your body. Find the places that are holding pain and release it. Choose to live a Life of gifts. Choose before it is too late. Be the Love you need.

༄

Making a choice involves choosing one thing and not choosing another—I can't have both things at once. Once I choose, it's impossible to know exactly what the outcome of the other choice would have been. The following conversation came in response to my considering whether or not I should use a medication prescribed to me. I was skeptical. The Teacher who arrived was a small, wiry Chinese elder. He was dressed simply in loose cotton clothing and had a thin grey beard.

Lao-Tzu:[24] *There is nothing that is really so black and white, so clearly this or that, as you would like to think it can be. You have seen that this chemical helps you and also has side effects. That could be said about every action that you take, every thought that you have.*
One difference here is that I am very consciously choosing when and how and if to use it. I could also choose not to.
Do you really think that you are not choosing other things?
Some things I am unaware of choosing, or am unaware that I have a choice.
But you do. Everything is a choice. Everything has a benefit and a drawback. Balance is the goal. Too much benefit leads to attachment and greed. Too little benefit leads to suffering.
And, are my choices spirit-fueled or ego-driven?
Again, you are living in a human form, so it is difficult for something to be just one of those. But, yes, this is the basic question. Are you using your choice to create harmony and balance. You may begin one way and then find that you have gone down another path that is not so. There is constant need of correction.
    We are not going to tell you what to do here. Learn to observe yourself and make your own measurements.
But how would I know the outcome of the thing I did not choose? I can only guess. Oh, I can evaluate the choice I *did* make, and use that to inform my patterns of behavior.
Yes. Are you spiritually connected, present, within the moment? Has your choice, whatever it is, made that possible or inhibited it?
    You do not want to be observing your behavior as if you are outside of yourself. This can lead to judging. You will want to look at the vibration created, and what effect that vibration has on your presence. Ultimately, you want to be both in the present and detached from Ego.

---

[24] This is the name he gave when I asked. It feels arrogant to report that I have been talking with such an esteemed Teacher, but it is the truth. What do I write down? He is motioning to the text and says, "go ahead, put my name down."

Although all of our choices ultimately affect our life's trajectory, some of the choices seem monumental. When I first began my path as an author, I had no idea what I was doing. There were many choices to be made in areas I knew nothing about, and I felt overwhelmed. A Teacher came to me in a vision to help with that process.

In the vision, I saw the strong hand of an elder. I recognized that hand as belonging to my mother's mother, long gone into the Spirit World. She curved her finger, motioning for me to come. I felt a soft bump as my energy presence met hers. I smelled the memory of her essence, which was comforting. I leaned into her presence and felt safe, secure. I am resting against her chest and she has her arms around me.

Grandmother Martha: *You are going to be alright,* she says, stroking my hair. *You are taking a big step in the physical world. Recognize that you are also taking another step in the Spirit World. You will be connecting with other physical beings who are walking both worlds.*

You are afraid of the new world you are entering. You have been doing this work in isolation so far. You will need to partner, and trust others. This is difficult for you. Sometimes it is hard to know someone's intentions. We are going to help you with this. Sometimes you will not understand why we are guiding you in a certain direction. You can trust us. You have a bigger picture available.

You are both afraid of and attracted to this power. You are just new at managing it. We are going to help you make decisions. So far, things are going well. The physical object of the book is going to be created. The first of many steps along this path. Yes, you are telling yourself to be open to opportunities. How will you know which things to choose? Keep checking in. Trust your Spirit Guides. You know how to do this.

You are asking about others—are they a distraction or a part of the picture? They are both. As long as you are working on spiritual development, they are helping. When it falls into social neediness then it is distracting. You know this. How do you sort that out? You need to set aside regular time to discuss spiritual matters with them. Be clear that that is what you are doing. Show them the book. Help them understand that this is your focus. You cannot give yourself away in a relationship. Be aware of when you are compromising yourself.

The project is important. It is not more important than your life. Your life is what supports the project, makes it possible. Making your life vibrant and productive is something that you are in charge of. We cannot make those decisions for you. It is important to be living your Life. That is what you are here for. Creating the books and moving them through the world needs to be something that enriches your life. It can't be detracting from that or reducing your energy. Then you can be sure that you are moving in exactly the direction you need to. Let go of needing to know.

The choices I make don't happen in a vacuum. Everyone around me is choosing, too. Life is one enormous, messy, beautiful, frustrating and fascinating experience in human-ness.

Universal Wisdom: *You want things to be very neat and easily analyzed. But this is about human beings, who are more complex than that. Even you can not be boiled down to a formula. A person can only function within their skill set. Some people have fewer emotional skills, because that part of them has been restricted. It's like foot binding. The individual ends up crippled, in a way. And that disability is important to keep in mind, because it's not pleasurable for them, either. It is painful and frustrating and humiliating, especially when others have so many more skills. In that way, silence is a skill, because it is a way they have learned. It's not the way we come into the world, it's something we learn to do.*

Different people have different experiences and gifts and skills. We're not all the same. It may be helpful to know that there is a purpose to our differences.

A'riquea: *One reason that Life is made this way is so that each person can have a unique energy impression. No two people will be the same. Everyone has gifts and losses. Your work while you are in human form is to use your unique energy impression in the best way possible.*

This involves finding your spiritual passion and expressing it through compassion. The way in which you make your way through your own unique energy maze leaves an energy impression on the Universe. This is what is meant when it is said that your learning goes back to the One.

Everything that everyone is learning in physical form is available in the infinite energy field of the Universe. You contribute to it and you are bathed in it. You have access to it. There is not a separate individual in the world. The energy is in constant motion.

Humans are often distracted by the desires of the physical form. This kind of information is like chatter, like static on a radio station. In order to access the inclusive field of all energy, humans will need to find themselves in the field of All-That-Is. This is like tuning in to a radio station. You are more likely to be a good listener if you are a clear channel.

You are wondering where love fits into this. Little-L love is the opportunity for humans to express and receive the vibration of big-L Love. There really is no difference between the two. Humans, however, are always practicing. Mistakes are made. The love/Love is given and withdrawn, it bathes and then dries up. The challenge of the receiver is to be open to the Love of others, and then to stay open even when it is removed. The ego tends to see the removal as a personal threat, and tries to build protection against the pain that is felt.

Everyone, on their human journey, has to figure out how to become open to the Love of the Universe. This is the greatest Love, and it is unconditional. It is always present. Once this is experienced, it is easier to forgive the imperfections of other humans. Early unconditional love from a parent or caregiver boosts a baby's ability to recognize spiritual Love. This can also be a barrier to discovering Universal Love in adulthood, if the person comes to believe that this Love always comes from another person.

Only under significant circumstances can another human provide truly unconditional love. Being parented without unconditional love can encourage a child to put up barriers, but it can also enhance the ability to find spiritual Love in the Universe, outside of their strings-attached relationships with others. So you see, it is not that one way is better than the other. It is up to each person to find their way within their own circumstances. The circumstances are all different. The outcome—opening to spiritual Love—is the same.

This is a good application of the One Mountain idea: some people are walking, some are riding a donkey, but everyone is climbing the same mountain. We cannot judge others for the way they are traveling. We can smile when we meet them on the way. Have joy in your heart at the opportunity to make this journey. Believe, in the Love of the Universe, and in the journey that opens to it.

Everyone is on their own journey of learning. Every one of us has a purpose in being here on Earth.

Universal Wisdom: *You matter because you exist. Existing is not just a state of suspension in the physical world. Existing is a manifestation of the energy of the Universe, in a specific form. The purpose of this form is to effect as much positive energy as you can through this form, through this state. There are many ways to do this. The essence is the same, the expression varies.*

> "Don't be ashamed to be a human being, be proud!
> Inside you one vault after another opens endlessly.
> You'll never be complete, and that's as it should be."
> ~ *Tomas Transtromer*

Our ego would like us to believe that we are the only one struggling. Expanding our frame of reference helps us to see that everyone is struggling—it is part of human nature. We can reduce our challenges in life by stepping into this larger picture.

The Tibetan Buddhist meditative practice of Tonglen is an exercise that can help you deal with your feelings by moving them into a larger plane. It involves 'giving and taking,' or 'sending and receiving.' Tonglen is not a practice in transforming the feeling inside you. It is using your breath to just take in and send out. It is a way of loosening ego attachment by exchanging self with others.

Here is a simplified version:

> Begin by sitting quietly and becoming aware of your breath. Once you are relaxed, identify a reaction of your own that you find yourself dealing with on a regular basis. It could be anger, inadequacy, grief, fear, defensiveness, or some other feeling. Choose one. Take a moment to feel this feeling, to feel the vibration it produces in your body. Notice where in your body it is evident.
>
> Feel the feeling. Then imagine everyone in the world who is also feeling this feeling right now. With so many people in the world, there are likely thousands and thousands who are feeling this feeling right now.
>
> Take in this feeling, breathe it in.
>
> Breathe out, sending Love and Compassion to everyone who is feeling this feeling right now.
>
> Continue breathing in this feeling, and breathing out Love and Compassion for everyone feeling it. Practice this for a few minutes. Then include yourself in the everyone who is feeling this feeling right now.
>
> With practice, you can begin to understand *energetically* that you are not the only one with this feeling in this moment, and that there is room for both the feeling and also for Love and Compassion.

Once I see that being human is not something that only happens to me, that we are all in this together, it becomes possible to better understand another person's perspective.

> I had a very vivid dream one night that showed me this. In the dream, I was on an ocean coast. A sand beach came up to rocky cliffs, and I was traveling along the edges of the rocks. I had hiking boots on, and I was 'surfing' the rocks—easily sliding from one rock top to the next like I was on skis. I was going up and down among the rocks, but generally heading upward. I got to a high place and realized that I couldn't go forward anymore. There was a steep drop off, maybe 40 feet down or so. I was standing on the edge and rocks were crumbling away from under my feet.
>
> The moment I turned to look behind me, intending to go

back, I noticed that a man had followed me there. He had quickly set up some kind of wooden framework. I couldn't fully see it behind the boulders. He looked disheveled and unkempt. The next thing I knew he was up on the rocks right behind me. He grabbed me and pulled me close. He was repulsive—his face was ashen grey, his greasy hair plastered to his head. His teeth were rotten and his breath foul. He was dirty. Clearly he had not taken off or washed his clothes for many months. He reeked.

I grabbed a rock in each hand to defend myself, but he anticipated my move and quickly had my arms pinned in such a way that when I moved my hands to hit him with the rocks, it strengthened his grip on my arms and kept them away. I looked over the cliff edge, considering throwing him that direction. Then I noticed a rope around his waist which was tied to the wooden structure below—there was no way he could get pulled over the edge. This was all premeditated. Then I noticed a second man, lower in the rocks, with his hat pulled down over his face. He was waiting to get in on the spoils. I was trapped.

The dirty man's face was touching mine and his putrid lips were reaching out to kiss me when I woke up. I was so creeped out that I felt, even while I was awake, physically dirty from the contact in the dream. It was 3 am, not time to get up. I couldn't shake the creepy intrusion, the vision of the filthy figure. I shouted out loud, "No!" and "Go away!" But nothing changed.

I decided to try something else. While I was awake, I went back into the dream and re-met the figure. Instead of fighting him, I entered his body to see out of his eyes. He was poor and homeless, a discarded human. He/we stood on a smooth rock looking out over the ocean and he stretched his arms wide and shouted out to the water. He was angry and hurt and hopeless. He felt that everyone in the whole world was against him. I recognized this sentiment as a piece of me. As a child, I had no steady place to live, no long-term relationships, no supportive family or mentors—no emotional Home.

This is the root of the defensive habits I still carry. I want to practice seeing this in my behavior now. Clearly, not everyone in the world is against me. Very few people in the world even *know* me. People are trying to be my friend. Some of them are making mistakes. We are all making mistakes. How do I let myself be trusting? A long time ago a teacher said *you don't trust the person, you trust the situation.* In other words, people are human. Things will happen that I can't control. But I can look for opportunities in the situation, opportunities for spiritual expansion. I don't have many people around me who can provide that. I am hungry for contact. I think that's actually what the man in my dream needed too.

"To be loved is wonderful, to be understood is profound."
~Ellen Degeneres

When I am able to take another's perspective, I can see that everyone is really just doing their best. I can see that the hurts and harms of my past are part of a shared spiritual journey. I can begin to forgive *human beings*.

The following is an ancient blessing that deals with forgiveness, affection, detachment, and liberation. It was originally created in Nahuatl, a native language of Mexico. It is helpful to say it aloud and with intention:

~I release my parents from the feeling that they have already failed me.

~I release my children from the need to bring pride to me; that they may write their own ways according to their hearts, that whisper all the time in their ears.

~I release my partner from the obligation to complete myself.

~I do not lack anything. I learn with all beings all the time.

-I thank my grandparents and forefathers and foremothers who have gathered so that I can breathe life today. I release them from past failures and unfulfilled desires, aware that they have done their best to resolve their situations within the consciousness they had at the moment. I honor you, I love you, and I recognize you as innocent.

-I am transparent before their eyes, so they know that I do not hide or owe anything other than being true to myself and to my very existence, that walking with the wisdom of the heart, I am aware that I fulfill my life project, free from visible and invisible family loyalties that might disturb my Peace and Happiness, which are my only responsibilities.

-I renounce the role of savior, of being one who unites or fulfills the expectations of others.

-Learning through, and only through, *love*, I bless my essence, my way of expressing, even though somebody may not understand me.

-I understand myself, because I alone have lived and experienced my history; because I know myself, I know who I am, what I feel, what I do and why I do it.

-I respect and approve myself.

-I honor the Divinity in me and in you.

-We are free.

Coming into the space where we honor the divinity in each other and ourselves is a beautiful experience. It creates cellular resonance, a harmonic, that joins us to the expanded Universe both within and without. It is important to recreate this vibration on a regular basis.

It informs our living not just during times of hope and beauty, but also in darkness and despair. Well-practiced, it becomes our way of Being.

I was a year out of cancer treatment and felt like I was getting my life back on some kind of track. All of my previous identities had been torn away by cancer. I had lost my career, my income, my social life, my physical health, body image, and sexuality. The one thing that was still intact, and in fact strengthened, was my spiritual life. I was peacefully sure of my purpose and my path.

Then an X-ray of a painful hip showed luminous spots. I had to entertain the possibility of metastasis—that the cancer had spread into my bones and throughout my body. Now I was no longer looking at the possibility of death, but the likelihood that I might be actively dying. In that moment, something shifted inside me. I felt as though I was squeezed through a tiny opening, pushed by fear and dread and acceptance and anger and exhaustion, pushed by circumstance and the limits of coping, into a space of complete openness. It was like fumbling along a small trail in dense woods and coming out into a broad meadow. A gift appeared spontaneously, and it was this song:

I'm traveling on my angel path,
I'm moving closer to God.
Feeling the welcome of the Spirits
I open my arms to heaven
I am received.

I'm traveling, my heart is certain
I see the beauty in each day
Offering gifts, making me Holy
I open my arms to heaven
I am received.

Soon after I was gifted with this song, **Mrs. Rogers**[25] appeared, encouraging me: *Well, there isn't much to be said right now. You had your heart touched by that church music and that's a good thing. I tried showin' you that a long time ago and maybe the time just wasn't ready yet. Anyway, you can keep on with that and you'll see where you go.*

There is something I would like to share, now. [She is stopping to think about it, her arms folded and a gloved finger moving across her lips.] *Yes, it could be the time for this.*

The world is a big place, you know. And there are a lot of kinds of people in it. That's for sure. But all those kinds of people really have one thing goin' together for 'em. They got this feelin' for what is good 'n right. There is no mistakin' that feelin.' It comes from right inside a person. It isn't even something you have to think about. It's just right there. That feeling was put there by God and no one else. That feeling is what comes when you know you are doin' right by God. That feelin' was put there so you would know *when you are doin' right by God.*

That feelin' is something that a person needs to find and to hold on to. A person needs to know what it's like to have that feelin,' to be right there where God is. It's the most important thing you can teach your children, to know about that feeling. To know where it comes from and where it's goin.' That feeling isn't somethin' that's stuck there. A feeling is somethin' that moves. *It comes from and it goes to. It comes from God and it goes in you. Then it comes from you and goes to someone else. When it moves like that it is also goin' to God. That's the way a circle moves. It's like what you been sayin' to those people you been marryin'.*

A circle has no beginning and no end, no giver and receiver, each is both the giver and the receiver.

Yep, something' like that. How that feelin', when it's movin', is just going 'round and 'round and 'round. But that's not all there is to it, that goin' 'round. When the feelin' is movin', and it's goin' 'round and 'round that

---

[25]**Mrs. Rogers** is a Black church elder from the 1960s. She wears Malcolm X glasses and is always dressed in her Sunday best, with a matching veiled hat and gloves. She can be stern, doesn't take no mess, but is always supportive.

circle (she's tracing a circle in the air with her finger), *then there is magnificence. Yep, write that: Magnificence. See, in that word there, it's like the word Magnify. And what does that mean, but to make somethin' bigger, to grow it. And doesn't Magnificence also make you think of somethin' glowin' and radiant? Those are the pure rays of God's Love.*

So you see, you got to move it. You got to find that place in you and move *it. When it sits still, it is not makin' any Magnificence. That would be like gettin' a birthday present and just throwin' it in the river. It doesn't make use of the gift and it sho' don't show any gratitude for it, neither.*

You had that right there in your song: "the beauty in each day, offering gifts and making me Holy." That is the Lord workin' in you. That is that place I am talkin' about. You got to be movin' that. You been disappointed in the chance that your cancer is back in your body. You were kinda tangled up in that idea of 'luminance.' You just gotta see that as Magnificence, that's all. You are *on your angel path. And so is everyone else in a body on this planet. All full of Magnificence. Open your eyes, children! Then your heart will open too. You got to be livin' it. Get going now!*
Thank you so much, Mrs. Rogers! Life is good.
Life is good. Life is God.

And *that* is the bigger picture, the whole infinite universal picture.

~ 4 ~

Empathy, Love and Compassion

Practicing expanded consciousness opens us up. It allows us to see ourselves and our relationships in The Bigger Picture. It creates an opportunity for us to see all beings in this larger context and experience the oneness of Being, where we are immersed in the energetic realms of empathy, Love and compassion.

Empathy is the ability to sense another's feelings. It requires that we open our perspective to include someone else's frame of reference. Empathy helps us care for each other—it is the social glue that has allowed the human community to grow and thrive over millennia. It connects us and creates movement toward compassion.

> "All human beings are members of one frame,
> Since all, at first, from the same essence came.
> When time afflicts a limb with pain
> The other limbs at rest cannot remain.
> If thou feel not for other's misery
> A human being is no name for thee."
> *- Saadi Shirazi* [26]

---

[26] This poem, by the Persian poet Saadi Shirazi of the 1200s CE, is written on the wall of the United Nations. It has been translated from Farsi.

Like most human characteristics, empathy is not the same from person to person—its expression is variable. The ability to imagine what someone else might be feeling has both intellectual and emotional aspects. The intellectual ability to understand how another person might react is called cognitive empathy, and the emotional ability to physically sense feelings is called affective empathy. Everyone has varying degrees of both cognitive and affective empathy.

At one end of the range, for example, psychopaths have high cognitive and low affective empathy. They are very good at understanding how others might react but not very good at sensing feelings. They don't read others' distress or experience discomfort at the negative consequences that their own behavior creates. Because their actions are not limited by feelings, they may purposely use their cognitive knowledge to manipulate others.

By comparison, people with autism are on the opposite end of the range. They have high affective and low cognitive empathy. They are capable of sensing emotions and feeling empathy for others, but they have difficulty navigating the social rules that would prevent them from hurting others. The harm their actions cause may be unintentional.

Most people fall somewhere along the spectrum between these two poles. Even gender can affect empathy. Men tend to have lower empathy, probably because over the length of history they have been required to hunt animals and go to war. Women tend to have higher empathy, likely because they bear children and have socialized every generation of humans. We are talking in broad generalizations, of course. Every person is different, and it's important to keep this in mind during our interactions with friends, family, and strangers—we're not all on the same empathy page.

෴

I am a sensitive person. I shudder when I hit a butterfly with my car. I generally know how a person is feeling when they walk into the room. I am seen as a good listener, and am regularly sought out by people who need to talk. Graphic scenes in the news haunt me for weeks, months, even years—I have learned to just not look at them. I am an empath.

An empath is a person with both high affective and high cognitive empathy. An empath has the ability to easily sense the mental or emotional state of others. If you are reading this book you are probably an empath, too. On a personal level, being an empath is a wonderful gift. Empaths are able to understand other people in a way that helps them feel seen and understood. Don't we all want that? To be seen and accepted for who we are? It's comforting and helpful. It builds harmony.

Being an empath can be problematic, however, when I forget or am unable to safeguard my own boundaries. I become a magnet for people who need to tell their stories. These conversations are heavily weighted towards the other person, without much give and take—it's just them talking and me listening. I sometimes have trouble recognizing the limits of my own time and energy in these situations. It can be exhausting. I also need to be able to listen to these stories, which are often sad and trauma-filled, without absorbing that energy into my being—to be less of a sponge. Would that mean that I give less?

There is a constant barrage of conflict being broadcast through the news. I feel the need to maintain worldly awareness, but that invites a constant stream of trauma. How do I actively participate in being human while maintaining my emotional health? Do I have to care less? Would I even be able to do that?

I need to somehow develop filters, to care for myself and allow things to flow by. How do I manage being an empath? How do I stay spiritually open to Love and still maintain healthy boundaries?

A'riquea: *There are terrible things happening all over the world. You are only aware of small numbers of those occurrences, and then only through social media. These things have been happening for millennia. They are happening on the personal level, community level, national and global level. Your distress is a beacon, reminding you to mind your* *own energy and what you put out into the world. You cannot change these large-scale events. You can only be mindful of yourself.*

There are also beautiful and loving things happening simultaneously, on the personal and community and national and global levels. Think of all the people who are not incarcerated or oppressed, or who are but are still managing to love those around them. People are loving each other. All the time. It's not that you should not fight against injustice, but the broader directive is to Love One Another. Your distress is a sign that you love these people and care about them. It's important to understand the context of your living.

Cognitive empathy can also be called 'perspective taking.' In order to understand each other, it is vital that we leave our own frame of reference to see another's point of view. If we are unable, then we will easily judge and dismiss others. We will hold biases (both known and unknown) against those with a different skin color or gender expression, or those from another culture or religion or economic condition.

This is the source of our cultural divisions today. People who have been oppressed are speaking out and our society is taking a closer look at the sources of their pain. Those who don't have the emotional skills for this examination retreat into their own place of safety, blaming the oppressed for the distress. They see the oppressed as threatening their identity or status and lash out against them. That is the opposite of cognitive empathy. It's the kind of me-first thinking that ego thrives on.

Ego wants to be seen as something special and important. It wants to set itself apart from others. These habits create exclusion. Our personal relationships are often mired in ego, in defense of our identity.

A'riquea: *Personal relationships, for the most part, are a distraction. They provide learning opportunities, but are not a place to get stuck. Look for the path, recognize when you are on it and when you are not. Being is Opening. Practice Being.*

The important thing is to be able to recognize what is important and what is just a distraction. Spirit knows what is core and what is not. You must ask Spirit to be your guide. Being open means being open to Spirit—your own and that of others. Don't be so concerned with who is paying attention or not. Be concerned about whether you are paying attention, or not. Love the world. Be in it. Be it.

Loving the world means that I value all beings. As an empath, I feel so much emotional empathy for others that it can sometimes be physically painful. It's hard for me to believe that someone else doesn't feel the same way, that they can turn away from the suffering of others. Yet I sometimes have to turn away too, because the pain is more than I can tolerate. Or someone else's hate and fear are toxic. There is so much behavior to try to understand, both mine and others.

Universal Wisdom: *These are difficult times for humans. Everything that is happening all over the world is being broadcast instantly into your home environment. This can be overwhelming. It is important to be able to step away and put things in context. When there is negativity, it is easy to react by being negative also.*

I am often distressed by the idea that my country seems to be heading down a Stalin-esque path. There is so much fear everywhere. Fear for what is going to happen. Fear of speaking out against it. Fear of not speaking out.

In the bigger picture, what has happened is a little blip on the radar. In the bigger picture, the fear that led to this outcome is actually the energy disturbance of the nearby Shift. We have been talking about this for some time. People feel uneasy and they need a place to locate that uneasiness. It manifests as fear because the future is an unknown. As a cancer survivor, you understand that the future is always unknown, but not everyone has this perception.

You are asking if there is some way you can use your skills to guide or support healthier change. The answer is Yes and No. You cannot change the minds of those who are not ready. They will go the way they have been going. You may be able to change the minds of some who are on the edge of change.

You cannot move forward with the idea that you can or will make change. That only sets you up to have your ego take over. You can use yourself as a model, of a way to be. It's not really important how big of a wave this makes. What is important is how many are making this kind of wave. As you have learned, there is a collective wave of change. The small changes can collect into a bigger change. This is the effect you can have on your own.

If you want to have a larger effect, you will have to look for the places where the waves are already moving, and connect to those. You need to be following your own path at the same time. That is what you can do. Follow your own path and your own purpose.

It is important to point out negative behavior when you see it or are exposed to it. And how you do that is very important. You can not become a hater of haters. You have to become a lover of those the haters hate, and even a lover of the haters. Not a lover of the haters' behavior, but a lover of the haters themselves. You must be a lover. A Love-er. That is your purpose.

I have often felt that I could love *any*one. Empaths are like that. We're typically a product of the school of hard knocks, which makes it easier for us to understand the suffering of others. But our experiences also tend to leave us with holes in our energy boundaries. We become porous. We become overly involved in outside situations, taking in and taking on the suffering of others.

A'riquea: *All of the situations that you are concerned with each have their own flow, regardless of your interaction with them. They are happening right now, just as your life is, and everyone is doing their best with what they have.*

You have taken on the role of Fixer, and you are applying it in all of these situations. That is not your job. Your job is to live your own life with balance and ease, so that when you come into contact with these other lives you can offer the refreshment of less energy drain, for yourself and for them. Try to think of them as lives, not people. Then you will see that you are not in charge of them. People appear as Points in Time, while Lives are collections of moving Space. When lives intersect, you choose how your energy moves in that interaction. This is based on your own life path.

It is important to become aware of what is your business and what is not. You are in charge of your life. Other people are in charge of theirs. When you come to a difficult interaction, you will need to separate what is your business and what belongs to someone else. You can only address your business, your own energy intentions. Let go of trying to manage the business of others. When your energy is getting entangled, it is time to move on.

Taking on the business of others is not a good idea, because they will resent this attempt at controlling them, just as you would if they acted this way towards you.

Taking on the role of Fixer probably means that I think I know more about someone else's situation—and what would make it better—than they do. It's important to remember that I can't possibly know everything about another's frame of reference. As we've all heard, "You can't believe everything you think!" As an empath, I may be aware of another's distress, but I don't necessarily have all the information about what is causing it.

For example, my young daughter had moved far away from home when she called to wish me a Happy Mother's Day. She seemed irritable and short, and I assumed that recognizing her mother made her feel not-very-grown-up. It was not a satisfying conversation. I later found out that she had broken up with her boyfriend that very day, and she was trying to be considerate by not injecting her distress into our phone call. I sensed her feelings but was wrong about what caused them.

Feeling like I have a responsibility to fix everyone implies that I, single-handedly, can change another's direction. One teacher had this to say about it:

A'dziimbuuma: *Who do you think you are? That you can just organize and control the outcome of the World?! There is so much energy swirling in so many directions that you cannot possibly even be aware of all that.*

Others are making decisions all the time that affect how the present lines up. Thinking you have control is a function of the ego.

Step back, energetically, from all of this pushing and fretting. When you relax into your spiritual core, you are opening Space around you. You are detaching from Points. You cannot be stuck in Points and also move in Space.

This is difficult, because the human world around you is concentrating on Points, correcting energy to keep maintaining the Points. Look around. It is spring now. You have been awed and humbled by the process of winter opening to green growth. It happens on its own time, doesn't it? When there is enough rain and heat, when the sun is high enough, the green comes. It shows up day by day by day, in little increments. Then one day, it is summer.

Everything has this cycle to it. It is all there. Everything is there in the Circle of Life. The circle is turning, in everything we do. In everything we are. Every step in the circle is also a cycle, a circle. There are many.

You are spending your energy worrying about putting things right, instead of getting your energy aligned with The Circle. Let yourself feel The Circle. Join The Circle and turn the Wheel of Life in all you do. That is the Red Road, the Good Way, the Christ Path, the One With All. It is why you are here. To do just this.

Let the distractions fall away. Focus on Space and opening. That is how you keep the path free for opportunity.

༄

Changing my energy focus requires attention to its location. It's not so much about moving it away from stress, but about actively moving it toward relaxation and openness. I understand this cognitively, but putting it into practice is not so easy. I am constantly being pulled in different directions. There are many situations which seem within my scope of management but are basically out of my control.

At one point, for example, I was a single mother and my daughter was diagnosed with a significant medical condition. She was a teenager and had difficulty seeing the importance of long-term self-management. At the same time, my elderly father was falling into dementia. He was living alone, failing to navigate the complexities of medical care, and refusing any help. Either one of those crises was enough to sap my energy, but I was dealing with both in addition to the fatigue of my own cancer treatment and the related financial hit of losing my job. I wasn't sleeping or eating well. I wasn't able to exercise or rest. I was completely stressed out. Absolutely no one was benefiting from my stress.

What is this stress, anyway? It's worrying about a future that hasn't happened yet. It's taking on more than belongs to me. It's not putting context around these situations. Clearly, it's about not being present.

Universal Wisdom: *This is one of the more difficult things about being human. There are so many feelings to deal with. If you are a sensitive person, and you* are *a sensitive person, then you easily sense another's distress. You have a hard time delineating what is your own stress and what is someone else's. You cannot relieve someone's stress by taking it on yourself. Certainly not by adding yours to theirs. Having a stress reaction is adding to their stress, whether you are in close proximity or not.*

This is about the energy vibrations you create. You can help yourself be more present, to yourself and others, by paying attention to the energy of your being. Take a minute now to scan your body, and see where you are holding your energy. If you are feeling stressed in some way, then your energy is probably concentrated in your upper body and your head. This kind of arrangement places you off-balance. Literally. Your upper body is heavier than your lower body, and your muscles need to tighten to keep your energy-self from tipping over. Bringing your energy lower in your body, into your pelvis or belly, creates more stability and freedom of movement.

I invite you to join me in a breathing exercise. This is a little energy practice that you can do anywhere, any time, for any amount of time: Try to breathe, not just with your lungs, but with your energy. When you breathe in, let your energy move into all the space inside your body. When you breathe out, let your energy move into all of the space around

your body. Focus on your torso, the trunk of your body that includes your heart and your belly.
Close your eyes now. Try to breathe, not just with your lungs, but with your energy. When you breathe in, let your energy move into all the space inside your body. When you breathe out, let your energy move into all of the space around your body.
Breathe in, breathe out.
Feel the energy inside your body, feel the energy outside your body. Concentrate it. Expand it.
Breathe in, breathe out.
Experience density, experience freedom.
Bring it in, let it out.
Breathe in, breathe out.

This breathing exercise returns me to my place in the Universe. It reminds me to let go of Points and rejoin the flow of Zone.

Aligning my energy in order to care for others means also taking good care of *myself*. I have to take care of my physical and emotional and mental and spiritual body so I can actually be present.

    I became keenly aware of this in the aftermath of cancer treatment. My energy had a very low ceiling. The only way I could manage was to reset my expectation of how much I could accomplish in one day, or even one hour. I had to bring down my energy output to match the energy available. I had to slow down and take care of myself.

    This was something like a monastic life. It removed me from the hustle and bustle of busy expectations. It immersed me in the pace of a spiritually-focused life. That is certainly the model that I am trying to teach: resting my attention only on the things that really fit my path and letting other distractions fall away by not giving them my energy, being more in the present.

Universal Wisdom: *Be selfish. Be who you are and take care of that being. You have been reduced to ground zero. Live there. Take your* *time. You are on a path of destruction if you do not listen to your own needs. It doesn't matter how they match up with your expectations or those of others. Let yourself Be.*

From a spiritual standpoint, I know I am here to witness others, to say "I see you and I Love you," regardless of their behavior. Stepping back in this way gets my ego out of the picture. I also have a need to be seen and loved just the way *I* am, and to be more than just a therapy support for the whole world. To develop better relationships, I am looking for better ways to interact.

I can hear echoes from a previous teaching: we go to great lengths to make sure that everything in life is harmonious when, of course, it is not. Other people make choices and we experience the consequences.

A'riquea: *It is true that other people make choices. Everyone is choosing, all day long, and doing their best with the skills and the means they have. You will want to recognize when someone is making a choice that affects you badly. You can recognize that choice and then make a statement about how it is affecting you. You can give them the opportunity to make changes.*

When you turn yourself inside out trying to adapt to their behavior, you are not being true to yourself. You are presenting a face that you think will help the other person. If it is not helping you, then it is not helping them, either. That is a sideways form of dishonesty.

You are the way you are because of your nature and your upbringing. Other people have their own construct. We are all many layers of many interconnected lifetimes. I hear you saying that you do not like to have your existence discounted by others. Even that is a result of this construct—it is a pattern that you have experienced and that you know well.

In your relationship with your friend who seems to be hurting herself by making poor choices—that is her own construct at work. It is not your construct, and it is not your place to take it on. In your relationship with your friend who is very self-centered, that is her own construct from her own life. It is not yours.

Your job is to find the places where the constructs can meet, where they overlap, and enjoy those places, let them enrich your life and the life of the other person. When you find that the constructs are not in harmony, then you have a choice. You can engage in the difficult areas, and work towards a shift, or you can walk away and let them be.

You tend to have some black and white thinking on this. You wonder if you should walk away completely because of the difficult areas. They are predictable, aren't they? They are predictable in every relationship. That is the nature of human relationships.

One thing you can do is be more concrete about your own needs. You tend to think that everyone feels like you do, when they do not. You tend to think that other people understand your needs automatically, when they do not. It is up to you to state your needs, hopefully in a neutral tone that does not engage the other person's defenses. Imagine what you might say to each of these friends.

It is always a good idea to look at your own part of whatever difficulty there is in a relationship. That is ultimately how you decide to be in something or not. Stating your needs is the beginning of shifting a construct. It is always ongoing, a work in progress. You can tell how healthy the relationship is by how it progresses over time.

I didn't grow up in an environment that supported or guided emotions. Not just mine, but *any* feelings were seen as dangerous. I was taught to hide and ignore my feelings. I learned how to read a room and be careful, tactful and diplomatic. I learned to become invisible. As I developed the habit of focusing my energy on others, my boundaries became overly porous. Now I sometimes have trouble discerning which feelings are mine and which belong to someone else.

How can I step into my feelings now? How do I stand up in my own life? What function do my feelings have in spirit-motivated behavior?

Universal Wisdom: *Being in service to Spirit means that you are connected to the greater good of Love and Compassion. It is well and* *good to want to create that vibration for others. But it is incomplete unless you are also focusing that Love and Compassion on your own self.*

It is true that you have learned to stifle your feelings, as if they don't matter. It is not that you shouldn't feel hurt, because that is a signal that un-harmonious behavior is occurring. It is what you do with that signal that makes a difference. You can lash out at these uncomfortable feelings, but that only creates more disharmony. You can push the feelings down where they will not be seen, but this will affect your core, the place where harmony comes from.

It is important to find a way for these feelings to move without causing harm, to yourself or to others. First you must be able to acknowledge that the feelings are there. What are feelings, but chemical reactions to stimuli. Certain stimuli are familiar, and are likely to elicit a reaction.

I assume that the closer the person is to me, the more likely I will be vulnerable to the sensation of being hurt.

This is only partly true. Those close to you have the greatest chance of triggering feelings of any kind, both difficult and joyous. But strangers can be just as effective, in either direction. It has more to do with the familiarity of the reaction or the depth to which it affects you.

Expectations have something to do with this also. Sometimes you expect more communication, maybe even some thanks for your efforts. This is an important lesson in looking at why you choose any given activity. Are you looking for ego rewards, or spiritual rewards. This is not so simple. Most things have some mix of both.

We hear you wondering about a recent interaction.

There are certain dynamics in relationships that I cannot change. I've come a long way in understanding that. I'm not sure I can change how I feel about it. I *can* change how I react to it. The other person can feel however they want, but they don't get to tell me how to feel, or that my feelings aren't also important. Whether they know that or not, *I* have to know it.

People who irritate me with their personal judgment and disrespect give me a mirror to understand how I react to being dissed. It's knee-jerk. It comes from years and years and years of being criticized as a child—criticized for being my self, criticized for having feelings and needs, criticized for existing. I don't want the people close to me now deciding that I don't get to have feelings or needs. When they do this, it is obvious that *they* are uncomfortable in some way. They lack the ability to deal with it. I am tired of behaving as if that doesn't matter to me.

You have come a long way to recognize the difference between having feelings and reacting to them. There is another part to this that we would like you to think about.

You are wondering how you can travel in this world as such a sensitive person. You are deeply aware, sometimes painfully so, of others' feelings. This is a good thing. It puts you in position to understand many people and their actions.

Yet, it is difficult to feel so much all the time. It will be critical for you to be able to discern what is your feeling and what is someone else's. You think that you know this. But sometimes you are absorbing things that don't belong to you. Your recent interaction is a good example. While it is true that there is family history and dynamics at work, it does not have to be the under pinning of every interaction and reaction. You do not know what that person's day was like, or even what their childhood was like. They are reacting just as you are reacting.

It is tricky business to sort this out, especially when you are so sensitive. Save your reaction for a few days, and see how you feel over time. It's not that the immediate feelings are wrong. There are no wrong feelings. But you may feel differently over time. If you still feel strongly, without feeding the feelings, then it may be time to say something.

Can you give me some more information about how to function with high sensitivity?

This will come in time. You are learning much about how to function in this life. Patience is needed. There is always more to come. Always.

I am thinking of the four skills you encouraged in another teaching: Triumph, Humility, Acceptance, Laughter.[27]

---

[27] These skills are outlined in *Traveling Light*, p. 159-60.

Add Love. This is the value that must be present in everything you do. For others, for yourself.

༄

The beauty of adding Love came home to me in a very stressful situation. I had traveled out of the country to visit my 20-year-old daughter. While I was there it became obvious that she was very very ill. She was in extreme pain and bleeding internally. We ended up in the Emergency Room, waiting on metal folding chairs in a crowded hallway while witnessing other unattended emergencies as well as violent interactions between psych patients and law enforcement. After nine long hours, we went home at 3 a.m. with nothing but a doctor's referral for several days in the future.

It was hard to feel so powerless, to watch my child suffer, weaken and fade away. She lost 20 pounds in 10 days. I struggled with guilt—could this have been prevented? I felt frantic and panicky, witnessing her deterioration right before my eyes. As a trained nurse, I racked my brain for possible actions or solutions. My mind raced to the future and any likely complications. I wept. I couldn't eat. I couldn't sleep. *I* started deteriorating.

I was aware that taking on so much stress was depleting me as a person and as a parent, and I needed to be well in order to support her. The best thing I could do was accept that I am powerless to change the physical disease. The power I do have is to love and support my child, and I did the best I could with that. I know she feels it. That is what is important. That she doesn't feel abandoned or misunderstood or uncared for, that she doesn't have to do this by herself. This makes me cry. I wish Love alone could heal her.

I asked the Teachers if there was anything else I could be thinking about or doing.
There is something you could do. And that would be to let the world be itself. Everything is moving. When you concentrate on pain and suffering, you create energy clots, you tighten the energy and reduce the flow.
I've been doing that to my own body and my own energy. It was helpful to teach a workshop today, to be reminded of what it feels

like to be in flow.

But you are still focusing on the negative. What could you find that would be positive about your daughter's situation?

Hmm. That's tough. I got a real-life eyeful of a big city emergency room. My daughter got connected with a highly skilled specialist. I managed to come together with my dysfunctional ex to co-parent, something I would never even have considered before. I reached out and connected with another mother whose daughter has this same condition. I learned that one of the best ways to deal with powerlessness is to accept it. I gave my daughter the purest love I could, just because she needed it.

That last thing is the most important. Say it again.

I gave my daughter the purest love I could. In the end, other than being with her and helping her stay on track medically, it was the most important thing I could do. Give love. Be Present.

In the end, it's all you can do for anybody. You cannot fix their pain, you cannot right their wrongs. You have spent your life trying to save people, when all you can really do is Love them. Your goal in maintaining or creating flow is to make the environment where the most Love is possible. You can do this. Anyone can do this. It's why you clear your own baggage, it's why you step aside from your ego. It's what integrity is. It's what a life of substance is.

It's not holding on to Points and pinning down time and energy. It's releasing the Points, using them for reference only, as you move energy through Space. That energy is Love. We cannot say it enough. That energy is Love. It is Multi-Dimensional Positive Energy.

That's all you need to know. You are in a low energy state. You cannot hold everything you usually do. The only thing you need to feel is Love. Let yourself Be Love. Uncomplicated. Plain. Easy. Free. Who you are on your most basic level. Beyond Ego. Beyond even the thought of Ego. Pure Spirit.

That is the gift of this exchange. You have whittled away everything to expose Spirit. It is beautiful. You are beautiful. Life is beautiful. Give thanks.

Praise Be.

Who is this? I thought it was Universal Wisdom, but I hear a deep voice. I see a Black man with a broad face, a big smile, and an easy laugh.
I'm going to the same church as you.
[This makes me smile.]
The Universal Church of Love and Compassion.
I keep hearing the word '**Mister**'
That's right. Just call me that.
Thank you.

This lesson showed up again in a different circumstance. With climate change, the area where I live is becoming hotter and drier. During a summer of extreme drought, we did not have any rain for three months. Forest fires raged nearby and the crews that fought them were stretched thin. Any spark could start a new fire anywhere at any time and there would be no one to come and help.

Since I have no running water I did not even have a hose available. I was in position to possibly lose my home at any moment. I had to create an evacuation plan. I moved important documents and a few heirlooms to a safer location. I packed my car with essentials, ready to go.

The forest around me became sere and brittle. The trees were stressed, their leaves curling and yellow, falling to the ground in July like it was September. I was standing in my smoke-filled yard as ash floated down from the sky. I looked up at the trees and felt distressed for them. I cried in helplessness.

In that moment, I realized that adding my distress to theirs was not helpful. What they needed was my love and positive energy. From then on, I stood regularly among my trees and offered, not stress, but Love. That's what I needed, too. That's what anyone in a stressful situation needs—Love and positive support.

Practicing Love and positive support has become more difficult as many interactions, whether with family members or strangers, have become fraught with stress fueled by social media and political incivility. The Teachers previously explained a technique for creating deeper conversation called "Go First." It involves steering a conversation toward compassion by going first, by sharing myself through a deeper idea and asking the other person for a response.

A'riquea: *It will be important to consider the topic and leave it broad enough for the other person to form their own ideas to share. But there is another way. You can also bring your own concerns to this person and ask them for suggestions or support.*

People like to feel like they are being helpful. It gives them meaning and purpose. Asking is a state of vulnerability, which shows that you are willing to leave space for whatever comes into it. Discussion is good, but bringing up a specific topic assumes that you already have an idea about it. Asking for assistance creates more space. It's less linear than a discussion. It's more freeing. What would you ask for if you needed help?

I can see right away how this makes me more vulnerable. It's a little scary. But it's also what I'm asking the other person to do.

Think about the words you use. What and When and Where are more specific, imply a more linear answer. How, and Who, can be more spacial. Starting with Please Help Me creates an invitation. Starting with naming a problem is generally a way to inspire defensive response, or pushing away. What you want to do is inspire movement toward each other, creating common ground, a place where you can stand together. Assurance is helpful: I want to be with you, I want to be With you.

Make sure you are truly "seeing" the other person. Give them space to be seen and Loved. Compassion is not an action aimed at another person, it is a space created between you where your spirits can meet and resonate together. You must be open to this if you want the other person to open, too.

Yes, this is a lot like therapeutic relationships. All of our relationships could be therapeutic, creating positive energy every time we engage with someone else. Therapy in this sense is not about a Healer and a Person Being Healed. It is about Healing Relationships, in which both people share. It does not mean absorbing the other person's energy, it means creating a space where your energy can meet. And if your center is grounded in spiritual vibration, you will not only tolerate this but go away enriched through the sharing, the resonance. It takes practice.

Creating a shared space where our energies meet is evidence of compassion. Compassion is like water:

> "Water is a mutable element. It changes shape with each contact it makes. It is its own self and it also becomes that which it touches. This is the way of compassion—to be one's self and also recognize one's self in the other. Compassion is evidence of Life Force."[28]

Empathy is a feeling. It's sensing how someone feels and trying to imagine how that might feel for you. It's a model of relating. Empathy is a gateway to compassion. Compassion is the awareness of another's distress combined with the intention to ease it. When it is unconditional, it is an expression of Love.

∽

For many of us, offering Love to others is much easier than loving ourselves. We struggle with the feeling that we are unloveable, and most of our addictions are attempts to get away from those uncomfortable feelings. The message that we are unloveable comes from so many different places. The media consistently tells us that we will never measure up. For a lot of people, the feeling of being unlovable comes from an internalized message that we have created, often based on the behavior of the people who were "supposed" to love us—our parents and caregivers. We have been taught that Love has to be earned. If we didn't receive it, then we must not have been worthy of it. But Love is always available. Our job is to figure out how to access it, how to open ourselves to it.

I did not grow up in an emotionally supportive family. I also had a

---

[28] **Darfur Grandmother**, in *Grandmother Dreams*, p.70

nomadic childhood, moving from state to state without an extended family or permanent community where I might have found a mentor. I learned skills like resilience, making the best with what I had, and managing on my own.

I've developed other skills. I can dance and bake and garden. I can maintain my car and fix a toilet and build a house. I can write books. But deep down, I sometimes still doubt whether I am capable or worthy, whether I could be loved. In those times, it seems that I am missing an inner confidence that comes with ongoing support, from being Loved. This has been an obstacle on my path.

Universal Wisdom: *When you have confidence in your own abilities and qualities, you will be able to find these positives in others as well. When you can focus on abilities and qualities in others, you will be less invested in their behavior. You will be less likely to be disappointed when someone behaves poorly. You will be able to see the behavior in the context of the whole person, not just one act.*

Of course, this also applies to you. When you are able to focus on your positive qualities and abilities, you will be less likely to judge an individual behavior of your own. You will be better able to separate Ego from Spirit.

This is difficult when you have been taught your whole life that you are a lesser person because of some trait that is not in your control: gender, skin color, body type, orientation, social class. You cannot become something you are not. But you can *become more of who you are. You can bring your positive qualities and abilities forward. You can nurture them and celebrate them. You can learn to appreciate them as uniquely yours.*

Everyone is good at something, at many things. We can learn to appreciate and support those many things in each person. That is what it means when you say "I see you"—you are seeing the real person inside the physical body, the spirit in the human temple.

Look in the mirror, look deeply into your own eyes and say "I see you." Say it with love and appreciation, with gratitude for the opportunity to apply your qualities and abilities in this lifetime. "I see you. I love you. I support you."

Say this to each person you meet. Say it with your energy and your presence, not necessarily with your voice, although that is good too. But you do not even need to know someone or interact with them directly to convey this gratitude.

For someone who is afraid to say these things to themselves, this is a good place to start, by loving others. It is a place to start, but not a substitute, for saying these things to yourself. You must become willing to take the gaze of self-Love. Not self-love, in the ego way of "I'm so wonderful." But self-Love, in the spirit way of "I am so full of wonder." Honor thyself as a companion of the Creator, ultimately unknowable except as an embodiment of the Universe.

This is not something to just think about. This is something to practice feeling. Open up, and feel the richness of Being.

Feel the richness of Being. Love is a vibration. It's like the wind, you can't see it, but you can feel it and see its effect. There is a small exercise we can do to help demonstrate this. I do this exercise when I am out walking in Nature.

I start by focusing my attention on just one thing. I might observe a mushroom nestled in the leaves of the forest floor, or a giant tree reaching high into the sky. My focus could be a river or a dewdrop, a flower petal or a mountain. It can also be done with another person or group of people, or for all of humanity.

Stop for a moment now and take three slow deep breaths. Think of some thing or some one that you would like to provide loving support for. Try not to choose something that is too big or that is a current source of difficulty. Choose someone or something that you would like to honor. Choose one that feels right to you.

Wherever it is that you choose, rest your awareness there. All you are doing is observing and feeling the energy of the other. Allow them to just be whatever or whoever they are. See their spirit. Quietly acknowledge their spirit. Express gratitude for their existence. Say to them: "I see you. I Love you. I support you."

Next, move your attention, and rest your awareness on yourself. Observe your own true spirit in the same way you recognized the other. Just allow it to be whatever it is. Express gratitude for your existence, for the opportunity to walk the Earth on a spiritual journey. Say to yourself: "I see you. I Love you. I support you."

Now, move your awareness to the space between you and the other, between the other and you. Recognize that your spirit and the spirit of the other are both existing in this space. The same space. Give thanks for this space, where everything exists.

Take a long, deep breath. Fill your lungs, taking in all of the space around you, and then let your lungs empty, into the space all around you. Smile. Repeat this slowly three times. Finish by rubbing your palms against each other to create a little heat. Place your palms together in prayer, on your chest with your thumbs resting on your heart. Say out loud: "Face to face, heart to heart, my spirit meets your spirit, in the space between us."

Everything in Nature is vibrating. Everything in the Universe is vibrating. Together, we are the vibration of The One.

Saying "I see you, I Love you, I support you," is an act of compassion. It is an active expression of Love. It is possible to practice the movement of this energy even under extremely difficult circumstances. I am going to share three very powerful and important dreams that demonstrate this kind of compassion. **Note:** Please be aware that the context of each dream is horrific and may be triggering.

In the first dream, I was living in a village in Europe in the 1940s and the Nazis had come. They had gathered up a small group of seven women, of which I was one. Each woman had been tightly bound to a tall sheaf of hay, a sheaf as big around as herself. The woman-sheaves were arranged in a circle, facing each other, and then the sheaves were bound to each other. The whole arrangement was bound to a platform on an open convoy truck, hanging off the back of it.

The sheaves had just been lit on fire and were beginning to

smolder. The smoke was wafting up from below. The women would not only be burned alive, but they would also watch each other burn alive. The plan was to drive this truck through the village to terrorize the other villagers.

At the last moment a young soldier in Nazi uniform, overwhelmed by his conscience, tried to intervene and stop the process. He was knocked out cold and his body was tossed into the center of the pyre, into the laps of the women. Then the truck drove off.

I was one of the women in that circle. I felt that my purpose, in that moment, was to remain calm and keep my eyes open. To look at each woman in the circle, look her in the eye, and say "I Love You" while we burned. No matter what evil was being thrust upon us from the outside, each person would die knowing they were seen and loved.

In the second dream, I was taken to a Nazi extermination camp in Poland. The prisoners were outdoors. It was early Spring. The sun was out, but the trees were still leafless and it was muddy and cold. I saw chimneys smoking in the distance and I smelled the sweet-foul stench of death. I noticed that the birds were singing cheerfully. I was being shown that even here, the world goes on and there is joy if you look for it.

I was brought over to the edge of a low concrete wall which was part of a large rectangle, like an old building foundation. It was a pit for the dead. The smell was awful. Just inside the wall lay an emaciated woman in a head scarf.[29] She was not dead yet, but she was dying. She was nothing but skin and bones. Her teeth and eyes seemed enormous, protruding from her skeletal face. I lifted her and took her in my arms like a baby, talking to her softly and kissing her cold cheek. She reached for me and tried to speak but could only mumble. I told her, "You are not alone, I am with you."

---

[29] I believe this woman is a relative of mine. I heard the name Olga Stephanovich, although I couldn't really make it out because I don't speak Polish.

We laid down together inside the concrete wall, side by side. I still held her in my arms as they began to shovel dirt over us. The soil smelled fresh and alive. I remember thinking that the dirt felt cold initially, but that our bodies (or mine, anyway) would soon warm it and then it would be like a nice blanket.

Then I realized that I was not dead or dying. I was not even a physical body—I was a spirit. I got up out of the pit with soil clinging to my coat and clothing. I sat outside the wall and held and stroked the woman's left arm and hand, the only part of her not covered by dirt.

Someone else's bony hand pointed over my shoulder to the nearby forest, which had suddenly transformed into the green of summer. Through an opening in the leaves I saw a beautiful young woman with dark hair. She was holding hands with a young man who was her beau. She was the dying woman in her younger years, now gone to heaven in her spirit body to meet her loving partner.

When I woke up I knew that, as a visiting spirit at the death pit, I had been able to ease her journey.

Both of these dreams are expressions of Love and compassion—the ability to behave with unconditional love toward others, whether in a physical or a spiritual body. We are also capable of directing this same level of compassion toward our self.

In the third dream, I was in the hall of some kind of school or office building. A man was pushing a woman around, slamming her against a wall. Concerned, I went over to intervene. His back was to me and over his shoulder her eyes flashed the desperate message "NO!" She was terrified, but knew that his rage would only increase if I tried to help her. He pushed her into a room and locked the door. I knew she was being violently raped.

I waited nearby until I saw him leave and then went looking for her. I found her lying flat on her back on the landing of a stairwell. A blanket covered her face and body. She looked like a corpse. I drew back the blanket. She could not still be alive. She had a plastic bag over her entire head and it was zip-tied shut around her neck. I removed the bag and she opened her eyes. They were a washed out blue, almost white, sunken and dried up, barely living. I said, "Let's go" and held out my hands. She took them and I helped her up. We began to leave. Then I woke up.

Her eyes. For days afterward I was magnetized by her eyes. Their black flash of magnified terror. The withered white orbs of her near-corpse. Yet she got up.

I am that person. I am both the body of the abuse survivor and the spirit of the one who waited for her.

The context I place on any of these three situations determines how I feel and react. If I limit my view to ego drama I will be frozen in terror, drowned by despair, or inflamed by rage. If I am able to step back and see this within the learning classroom of all eternal beings, I can stop and ask, "What needs to happen here? How can I contribute Love and Compassion?"

There are so many opportunities to choose this. Every time I encounter an unhoused person, for example, and feel drawn to bring them home with me. Or when someone shares their story of suffering and I end up taking on their suffering too. Or watching the world descend into the control of tyrannical bullies.

I cannot possibly be responsible for all of it. There are bigger players in history, with impacts bigger than any one person: Hitler or Putin; Mother Teresa or Martin Luther King, Jr.. None of these people could have been effective without the support of masses of people. I am one of many in the masses. I have a responsibility to not stand by, I cannot let fear prevent me from taking any action possible. But there are so many things vying for my attention!

A'riquea: *You could be less hard on yourself. You could decide that there is only so much one person can do. You can give yourself permission to make mistakes and walk away from them. You will find yourself in many situations where you have the opportunity to go down the rabbit hole of giving and fixing. You think you can be a savior. You cannot. You cannot fix people's individual lives for them.*
Look up the definition of compassion.

Compassion is sympathetic pity and concern for the sufferings or misfortunes of others. It comes from the Latin which means "to suffer with." To suffer with. I do not need more suffering. I have spent my life amassing suffering, my own and that of others. It is the bane of the empath, to keep building my store of suffering. Ah, there may be the problem: *storing* the suffering.
Exactly. You have been a collector of suffering, a hoarder even. This is wearing on your body and your psyche. It is not what is asked of you. It is good to understand suffering, as part of the human condition. It is important to be able to understand the suffering of others, to put yourself in their shoes and not judge what they are carrying. It is paramount to stand up for those who cannot stand up for themselves, to seek justice and better treatment. This is compassion.

Once you have made the connection to suffering, you must then be able to release it, to give it back to the greater energy of Everything. It is not yours to keep. That is like checking a book out of the library and never returning it. It is not your book, it belongs to everyone. It is there for everyone's use. You can renew it, but not indefinitely. Learn from books, then put them back. If you need to find it again, it will be on the shelf.

When you hold the book for too long, you are trying to make it part of your story, which it is not. It may have some resonance, some vibration that you relate to. But it is not your story. It is important to let go of stories that do not belong to you. This is important for the people whose stories they really are, who belong to those stories. Because if you really want to be a healer, you will need to have a clear heart. You will need to come from a clean place that is not crowded with stories that do not belong to you. You do this for yourself, for your own health, and you do this for others, who need you to be a safe place to touch and move on. This was one of your roles in the Native community, that you could understand their suffering but not be carrying it yourself.

You are not your suffering. That is an identity that clouds your Being. Free yourself of suffering, both your own and that of others. Do not ignore it, do not pretend it does not exist. Continue to read the Book of Life. Study the chapters that are helpful and apply them to your own situation. But then put the book back and remember to live in the moment. Live.

 Live. Gather. Release. Rest. This is the circle of life. The cycle of life. Do not get stuck in one place. Keep the circle moving. Keep moving on the circle. Energy flows from the turning of the circle. Energy stagnates in any one place or Point. Keep the circle turning.

Focusing on tragedy and dragging around its emotional baggage anchors me to Points. To keep the circle turning, I need to move my attention to Space, to the bigger picture which includes The Everything. Allowing my energy to vibrate with the Universe creates opportunities to honor my spiritual purpose and travel my Spirit Path.

Universal Wisdom: *It is good that you are becoming aligned. Also be aware that that alone is not going to move you along. You will need to be in harmony with outside factors in order to move along. You will be joining a flow that is bigger than you. This is not something you need to be concerned about right now. Continue to ready yourself. That is what you are doing now.*
Your job is to ready yourself and your support.
 This is the purpose which you have been given. It is meeting each person on their Soul Path and encouraging their Spirit, encouraging all Spirits, to come fully into the world and engage with it in a positive way. It is a Helper's path, but one where you share the journey too. Everyone is traveling together. Traveling spirits. The life of spiritual travel.

~ 5 ~

Heavenly Journeys

The Teachers are inviting us to practice expanded consciousness as a way of being. This benefits us personally, by reducing ego reaction and placing us in a larger context. It also benefits humanity and the cosmos, the greater good, by creating and increasing positive energy.

Expanded consciousness is a spiritual journey which occurs in everyday life. Everyone reading this book, for example, is a spiritual traveler. Just like going on a trip to some new location, spiritual travel opens our eyes. It stretches our psyche and rearranges our energy. We are transformed.

There are many ways to explore spiritual vibration. You may attend mosque or temple or church or another spiritual group. You may meditate, enjoy Nature, practice yoga, walk, create art. Spiritual energy is also moving when you show kindness to others, offer support, and volunteer in your community. Every one of these activities is a kind of spiritual travel.

There is one form of spiritual travel that every human will experience. There are many names for this journey: going home, walking the milky way, passing over, crossing the rainbow bridge, meeting your maker. Whatever name we give it, it means that our physical manifestation on this planet will come to an end.

Life is made of beginnings and endings. We experience this cycle every day of our lives. The sun comes up and a day begins. After a number of hours the Earth turns, the day ends, and night begins. We say that a day begins and a day ends. We *could* say that a day is born and a day dies. The time in between is a small lifetime, an opportunity, that arises and then ceases.

From the smallest to the largest, everything in life has this rhythm of beginning and ending. It doesn't matter if it's a day, a season, a cell, a breath, a project, or a lifetime. It begins, it is completed in some way, and then it ends—it transforms into something else.

> "This body is not me.
> I am not limited by this body.
> I am life without boundaries.
> I have never been born,
> and I have never died.
> Look at the ocean and the sky filled with stars,
> manifestations from my wondrous true mind.
> Since before time, I have been free.
> Birth and death are only doors through which we pass,
> sacred thresholds on our journey.
> Birth and death are a game of hide-and-seek.
> So laugh with me,
> hold my hand,
> let us say good-bye,
> say good-bye, to meet again soon.
> We met again tomorrow.
> We will meet at the source of every moment.
> We meet each other in all forms of life."
> ~ Thich Nhat Hanh

Every person in our lives is going to die, no matter their age or what kind of health they're in right now. Every single person on the planet is going to die—including those who haven't even been conceived yet. I'm going to die. My children are going to die. Every butterfly and bird and tree and mountain, every living thing will someday end. Absolutely nothing is permanent.

Death is a fact. The actual timing of our death is unknown, and that can be unsettling. What if we could approach this uncertainty, not with fear, but with curiosity? It's important to realize that we do have a choice in how we see death and dying, because our perspective affects how we experience life and living. Cancer was a beautiful gift for me because coming so close to dying made me more aware of *not* dying. Every day that I wake up is a good day, because what is the alternative? Not waking up? Every day is a good day because I get to have one more experience in physical form on this planet. I may not have tomorrow. But I have today.

Two friends are sitting at the end of a little dock, looking out at the water.
One says, thoughtfully, "We are all going to die some day."
The other answers, "Yes, but we get to live every day until then."

Before we make our final journey, we have the length of our lifetime to bring spiritual energy into the physical dimension, into the present. This is our purpose.
The Library Man is standing with his palms pressed together, a look of intent relaxation on his face: *This is one of the next steps, to see yourself in this arrangement, this more expansive dimension. It is a place where humans actually reside. This is how the human being is designed to function. This is the way that animals function in the world.*

Humans have gotten very adept at frontal thinking. It has crowded out the rest of the sensations of living. You, as a species, have come to the point where you have lost track of your actual location: you are a concentrated arrangement of energy traveling the physical plane of the Earth while the Earth travels through Space. This is all occurring in the context of the Universe, which is the Everything, including all Time frames and all locations. You have "materialized" in this moment. It can all change in a heartbeat, and you would be removed into some other location.

Humans fear this, this "death" if you will, of the physical dimension. It is the ego's job to stay attached to the physical domain, and it works tirelessly to maintain this. It makes sure that you eat, and protects you from injury and harm. This is the energy part of "you" that is most attached to the physical plane. Humans have grown to believe that this is all there is to their existence—food, sex, status, money.

The reason we are asking you to make The Shift, to recognize the broader energy context of your existence, that necessarily includes your spiritual manifestation, is because this is what is needed to bring the world back into Harmony. Native peoples knew about this balance, it was practiced in all areas of living.

Traditional cultures incorporated spiritual awareness, including knowledge of where we go when we leave our physical bodies behind, into their everyday living. **My Mother** came to me in a vision, using images to show me this place:

She motions for me to approach her and I am swallowed into her energy. I tumble gently in the deep darkness of a vast cave. Its sides are hard and rough and cool, moist with condensation. A little light reflects off the edges of the wet rock, and I turn to its source. It draws me to a large room in the cave where there is a very bright light. The light is coming from a great round opening in the floor. The light flickers white, and comes out of the round opening in a multitude of jets shooting straight up. It is a portal.

My mother looks at me a little mischievously with one finger to her lips, as if to say, *Shhh, I've got a secret.* She is amused. She turns away from me to look at the light portal. I walk over for a closer and see that each giant jet contains many small figures. They are mostly human in shape, some are animals. This reminds me of the Fire of Lost Souls,[30] but it is not a fire and there are no other beings standing around it. We are alone in a cave, the light is from

---

[30] The Fire of Lost Souls, as described in *Traveling Light* (p. 20-22), is a place for those who leave the physical plane but do not make a clear transition to the Spirit World. The Fire is an opportunity, after the body disintegrates, to help the spirit complete its full journey.

the jets and the beings are in the jets.

I am drawn to one of those small figures. It appears to be a man. I can't tell if he is heavy set or if the force of the jet is billowing out his clothing. He is floating on the stream of the jet. I look up to see where the jets are going. There is a hole in the top of the cave and beyond the hole I can see the night sky, clear and full of stars. Each jet dances up like a Northern Light, and its tip connects to a star far, far away. The jet is a shaft of light that plugs into the star, as if the star is a hole in the blue-black veil of the sky. The figures travel up the shaft and when they get to the place where the shaft enters the star, the figure passes through that star-opening into a brilliant white light on the other side.

I suddenly understand that this jet flow is the tunnel of white light that is seen in near-death experiences. With near-death, people come back. When someone actually dies they go through this opening into the brilliant white light of God and do not come back. They die physically and then their spirit travels on and does not come back to the body.

Where is the spirit traveling *to* when it goes through either the star opening or the Fire of Lost Souls? I have been there before. It's another realm. It contains worlds within worlds within worlds, just like this physical one. When we are able to travel there but stay in our bodies, many new things will open to us. Right now the people of Earth are locked into the fear of losing our physical bodies. This is part of the threat of climate change, that we will not have a physical place to live. There is nothing to fear because there will always be another place to go, another world within a world within a world. It will not be this exact one, but there *are* others.[31]

We should not give up our physical manifestation easily, because it is a gift. But neither should we cling to it, creating the energy clot of attachment. There is a place to rest our energy between

---

[31] For a fascinating account of what spirits do after leaving the physical body, see Helen Greaves' *Testimony of Light: An Extraordinary Message of Life After Death* (Tarcher/Penguin, 1969).

the wholly physical and the wholly spiritual. It is important to find this place, to practice being in this place, to practice Being. This is what we do in meditation, in centering, in letting go. This is transcendence, the world within worlds. It is lovely.

Many people have made this journey before us. For me to be born, I would need much more than two parents and four grandparents and eight great-grandparents. Genetically, my existence required more than 4,000 ancestors in just the last 400 years alone. The world of humans has been active for much longer than that—for hundreds of thousands of years. The ancestral math is daunting. But *all* of these people have come and gone ahead of us.

> "There's a million times more dead than living
> and the dead are dead a million times longer
> than the living are alive."
> ~ Flannery O'Connor

All of these people have come and gone ahead of us. They all had lives that left energy imprints in the universe. These are our ancestors, available to us through the expanded consciousness of channeling. There are so many of them and they have experienced so much. They are our elders. They are standing by to help us in our current lives on Earth, if we are able to listen.

In *The Spirit of Intimacy, Ancient Teachings in the Ways of Relationships,* Sobonfu E. Some says, "We might think that the confusion we experience in our daily life happens in isolation, but in reality it has something to do with our lack of connection to our ancestors....When we talk about connecting with the spirits of ancestors, many people assume that we refer to our own direct ancestors. But this is difficult. Many of us don't even know our grandfathers. There is such a thing as the pool of ancestors—it doesn't have to be a person or a spirit we know or can imagine. It can be the tree out there. It can be the crows out there, your dog or cat at home. Your great-great-grandfather who died many generations ago may have joined a great ensemble of spirits to the point where you can't even identify him. He's probably the creek running down over there....what is important is to realize that any person who has lost the physical body is a potential ancestor. And by simply expressing your longing for the support of ancestors, you will attract a lot of spirits. When you start a ritual where you need their support, if you address them simply as spirits or ancestors, maybe even say, "the ones who I know, the ones who I don't know, and those who know me more than I do myself," you are tapping the ancestral power out there, and you are not beginning with confusion as to whether in the pool of ancestors, there is a spirit out there than you can identity with."[32]

༄

The physical body and the spirit body join at birth, and this union dissolves at death.[33] When someone transforms through death, the energy of the spirit goes to "heaven"—it rejoins the energy of the universe. At transformation, our physical body does not just 'disappear.' Our bodies are constructed from the same elements as the Earth, and when we die the physical self disorganizes as a body and returns to its original elements.

Dancing in the pow-wow circle, I am acknowledging all those who have gone into the ground before me, who have lived a life that made my life possible. My toes gently kiss the ground in gratitude for their gift. When I dance in the pow-wow circle, my feet are not just touching the ground, my body is also in the air between steps. As I dance I am connecting the ground and the sky, Heaven and Earth, in my own body. There, the ancestors and I dance together.

One night at pow-wow, after everyone had finished their day and was quietly sleeping in their tents, **Migizi Niikaan** came

---

[32] Newleaf Publishing (Gill & Macmillan Ltd, 1999), p. 15-16.
[33] See *Traveling Light*, p. 10-17, for a detailed discussion of these transformations.

to me in a dream. I saw him disappear ahead of me through a hole into darkness and he asked me to follow. We came through a tunnel and out into a cave. Migizi Niikaan crossed the cave and climbed up onto a high shelf of rock on the other side. He asked me to follow. The shelf was a resting place for the ancestors, the ones who had passed on. What was left were their bones.

Migizi Niikaan carefully handed me a long bone. The bone guided me. I held the bone horizontally and pressed it to my forehead. I brought it to my lips and kissed it. I held it across my chest, my heart. I held it at my belly. Then I turned it vertically and held it against my shin. It matched my shin, and I knew that my own bones were the same as these bones. My bones are the gifts of my ancestors. I held the bone even with the ground, along my foot, and knew that when I dance, my ancestors are dancing also.

Bones are amazing. They are one of the hardest elements in our body. They provide the structure of our skeleton, while at the same time their soft insides create our blood. When I practice energy movement in the morning, I acknowledge the beautiful energy being created and emitted by all of my bones. Is there any more about this for me to hear?

Migizi Niikaan is before me, with his arms folded across his chest, one hand up and stroking his chin. He is looking at me thoughtfully. The hand on his chin points to the typing keys.

I took you to the bones because it is important that you understand the respect required in dancing. You have come to this in steps. First you understood the energy movement of turning the circle. This year you felt the shift, the gratitude for being alive.[34] *Now you will think about the gifts of your ancestors, and how to honor them in a good way. Life is short. It is important to enjoy it and use it well.*

---

[34] As I danced in the circle, I felt the circle turning and the healing of my body. After several turns, I also began to feel a huge gratitude for the opportunity to be on this Earth. I danced with joy and appreciation. I usually hear "kiss, kiss, kiss..." as my toes touch the ground in front of me. This time, I heard " thank, you, thank, you, thank you..."

I want you to know this: I want you to know that when this life is done, you will want to know why you did not appreciate it more. This is the reason that people are afraid to die. Their spirit knows that this is a limited opportunity. It seems so hard, but really it is so simple. To Love. That is all there is. To Love.

He motions to me that we are done. He smiles and jumps a little to his left, his head breaking the surface of something that has the qualities of water, even though it is a vertical surface. His body follows his head, splashing through that surface. He smiles and waves to me as he swims upward in the watery environment. I watch him go, as if I am watching through a plate glass window. He swims upward. He breaks through into the sky and becomes the bald eagle. The eagle flies upward, continuing his journey, higher and higher until he comes to the division between sky and space. Then the eagle passes through that divider in a burst of flames, and I see the white wisp of smoke that I have witnessed when other spirits leave their human bodies. The wisp of smoke remains visible momentarily and then dissipates until there is only the night sky, full of stars.

Now here I am, standing on what I think of as the surface of the Earth, which is really the bottom of an ocean of air. And the only thing I have to do is to Love.

All the days we are alive, we have this opportunity to live and to love. That window is always open. One day, the window of opportunity will close. The moment of death does mean that we will not come back into the same body again, but before death there is dying.

Everyone wants their death to be swift and painless. We want to go to sleep and not wake up. Statistically, only about three percent of us go that way. The other ninety-seven percent are going to decline over time and die slowly. Dying is a process. Note that the euphemisms we use for dying—crossing over, passing on, meeting our maker—are all verbs, they describe actions. Dying may look passive but it is an active process.

It reminds me of another doorway in life: being born. The baby needs to traverse a narrow passage that is designed to stretch slowly. The mother pushes and the baby's head advances. When she rests between contractions, the pressure eases and the head withdraws a little. Progress occurs inch by inch. Two steps forward, one step back. Two steps forward, one step back. It culminates in an event called birth, but being born is a process.

Our entire lives are marked by processes like this. We are working toward independence from the moment of conception. We grow and evolve until we are independent of the womb. We grow and evolve until we are independent of the breast, then the lap. We let go of our parent's hand and we start school. In adolescence we let go of our parent's home to make our own. Our task as adults is to let go of all the limits that have been layered over us along the way—the ego pressures of roles and identities, of cultural expectations. As an elder, we have the opportunity to let go of our Earthly journey and step into the next. Each of these steps is both an ending and a beginning. Life is a long series of these endings and beginnings.

∽

We may not have the opportunity to witness many deaths during our lifetime. Participation in this process has been sanitized out of Western culture, as if death is something to be hidden away and avoided. But dying is a very real part of living. Witnessing it may be painful and difficult. It can also be uplifting and inspiring.

As a nurse I have been present for the deaths of many people's family members, from newborns to elders, and in circumstances both serene and tragic. I have always considered it a blessing to be there for this transition. It's like standing in the moment where past and future dissolve into one, into the thin millisecond which is the present.

Personally, I have experienced the loss of several of my own babies and the sudden death of my mother. Then I was gifted with the experience of assisting my father in his dying process. Over nearly a year's time in hospice he declined gradually and I had many opportunities to grow.

I felt some distress when thinking ahead to my father's

passing. It wasn't that I felt uncomfortable with his body completing its journey, but I realized that his passing would create changes in my life, too. Now I would be the head of my own family. There would be no parent above me. I was transforming into a grandparent, an elder.

Great Grandfather: *We are moving with you. That is something that is often not seen. We are with you in the turning of the circle. Your ancestors do not leave you when you become an elder. You are coming closer to us. That is something to enjoy. The comfort of the ancestors.*

We are with you always. But sometimes in the passion of youth, you do not see us. Or you do not know how to look for us. But we are here. And you know us. We welcome you. We welcome your father. That is the beauty in witnessing dying. That you see your family member going back to the ancestors. Moving along because it is time. Transitioning. Letting go of the physical world.

You cannot imagine this, not quite. Because you are not there. Some day you will be. He is leading your way. That is why it is important to be present to the dying process. Because he wants to show you, he wants to be the leader. That is his way. And you honor him by honoring his way.

That is what is meant by being present with Grace. To let him lead the way, while you support how he does it. You must step outside of your own agenda and be the spirit-walking journey that will support him in the lightest and richest way. In that way, you will also be supported, and your own soul path will be shown. Illuminated.

As a female in a male-centered home I was seen as a lesser person, and my father and I did not have a close relationship. Initially, I struggled with the 'duty and obligation' of tending to him during his dying process. Over time, however, I realized that this responsibility to care for my elder was a holy journey for both of us.

Universal Wisdom: *This is the way Life is. Leaving is not as hard for the dying person as it is for the people around them. There is one thing you can do to help the situation: let it take its course. Do not take on the* *responsibility of rescuing anyone. All that does is keep them from doing their own work.*

What is my work here?

Your work is to bring that which is Holy to the surface, to help the Light of Love shine on this situation. This is not about trumpets and tambourines. It is a gentle rain on the soil of Living. It will help you to practice it, it will help others to feel it. This is what is meant by "Grace."

The word 'grace' comes from the Latin gratia, from gratus, meaning 'pleasing, thankful.' Grace is an expression of gratitude.

I knew that at some point the opportunities to be with my father would come to an end. He would pass and that would be that. I felt some inner pressure to make the most of what time there was. Many times I thought about the Tibetan practice of staying with the dying person and chanting. This is a practice that has continued over millennia. The chanting provides a vibration, a harmonic, a resonance that creates a path for onward travel.

I did not have the knowledge to practice such chanting, but by remaining in a meditative state I was privy to some of what my father was experiencing. This is one of the gifts of traveling beyond the five senses. It helped me understand his journey. It eliminated the worry of having to try to figure it out. There was no figuring to be done—only witnessing.

I was shown through images. Early in my father's process I saw my mother in the room. She had died two years earlier at the age of 83. In the first vision she was young and pretty, placidly sitting at the foot of my father's bed. She did not speak but started showing me various scenes. The first one was a snowy woods. She could change the scene by pinching her fingers together, making my whole field of vision open and close like a giant eye with the scene inside. She seemed to be going through the scenes until I chose one I liked.

I chose a scene of small birds singing and flitting in the branches of a tree. My mother's spirit entered that scene in another form, blending in lightly with the outline of the tree branches, the birds landing on her arms. The birds were not at all alarmed by her presence. They took it in as if she was part of all Nature. She *was* part of all Nature—she was showing me that there really is no difference between the worlds, that they are concurrent.

I asked her why she did not take my dad with her to the Spirit World. She looked out into the open field beyond the trees and there he was in his white pajama-underwear, running through the flowers and tall grass with his hair flowing and his arms extended out toward the sky. He was *running* there. She said, "He's not ready yet."

Over the course of his dying, this scene replayed several times. At one point I saw the field again. He was climbing down a wooden ladder from the field above, back down to his bed. He was leaving heaven and coming back. My mother was sitting in the field and looked a bit frustrated but kept her patience, letting him do whatever it was he needed to do.

It's clear that the field scene was an image of "heaven" being portrayed visually for me. It's interesting to note where my mother was—on the edge of the field or on the edge of the bed. There is an "above" and a "down here" quality, relative to the field and the bed. My dad's actions showed me where his spirit was traveling. At first he was running through heaven wildly, as if searching. Another time he was walking there calmly enjoying his surroundings. He always ended by climbing down the ladder back to the physical world. I did not have any influence on those situations. I was just an observer.

When is someone dying, and not living? Toward the end, I would've said that my father was living, but not in a way that seemed comfortable or meaningful for him. This is the process, the journey, that everyone will eventually make. He was just really taking his time. Whether that was his choice or his fate (or both), I'll never know.

After he'd been in hospice for many months, my father and I had an interesting conversation. He was not in any pain, but he was weak and confused. When he was restless and agitated he felt like he should go somewhere. The movies, a restaurant—the location varied but he was insistent that he had to go. When he'd had more energy I'd made several attempts to grant his wish and take him for a car ride. He was completely exhausted just by getting his coat on and could not go any further.

One time, after he had been talking about his mother, he insisted that he wanted to go "upstairs." There was no upstairs where he lived. We were sitting on the edge of the bed together. I took a risk and went down a different path. I told him that his mother and his wife were waiting for him upstairs, and he could go there but he would have to go without his body. He accepted this matter-of-factly. I asked him if he knew what I meant and he said Yes. He took my hand and held it. I told him that his father was there too. He said that his father had been gone for a very long time, so long that he couldn't remember him. I told him that his brothers would be there. I told him that he could go upstairs and I would come along later.

We talked for a little while about him going upstairs without his body. He knew what I was talking about but didn't know how to do it. I said that I didn't know either, that that was something he was going to have to figure out himself. I offered that maybe while he was sleeping, he was practicing going upstairs. He said that was true. He was tired, and he laid down then.

I got him tucked in and sat on the edge of the bed. He told me that he was worried about leaving his children. As a mother, I knew exactly what he meant—those are powerful Earthly bonds. I wanted to reassure him, however, that we would manage. I told him that his children would be okay because we had each other. That helped him relax, and he closed his eyes and fell asleep.

About 45 minutes later I poked my head into his room to check on him. His eyes popped open. He sounded surprised and disappointed that he was still on Earth when he exclaimed, "Nothing happened yet!"

I couldn't hurry my father's dying. I couldn't tell him how to make the journey. I could only be present to his process. Still, I wanted to be doing more than just changing sheets and emptying urinals. I wanted to be spiritually active. When I asked for direction a Teacher came to me.

A'riquea: *You will want to get the house in order. You have been doing that, in a very physical way. But there is another kind of house. It is the Nest of the Dead. This is the place where people rest after they die.*

I tried to do this a few weeks ago, with candles and meditations. It seemed to irritate him.

It is something you do for the other person, but not necessarily with them. It is an atmosphere, of lightening the load, clearing the way.

I'm not sure I understand what this would look like, what it would be.

It is not something that can be described in physical terms, because he is letting go of the physical world, isn't he? It is a clearing of the path, removing obstacles.

I thought that was up to him?

He is not capable of such direct action. He is ready to go, but his body is not.

I thought about this intriguing information for a day or so and I had many questions. To begin with, there is the idea that there is a place where the dead go to rest after they die. I usually think of death as an un-joining of the body and the spirit. The body goes into the ground or into the fire, and the spirit travels to other dimensions. But is there some in-between place where the person rests after they die?

Universal Wisdom: *You are getting trapped in the duality of body and spirit, of physical and spiritual, as if the two are somehow separate. You can think of them separately, but they are not. A person is an energy configuration. The configuration shifts over a person's lifetime, multiple times under myriad circumstances. The body is the house where these transformations take place, but all of the transformations are necessarily spiritual.*

You can begin to think of this like crystal structures. Water, for example, can take many forms depending on the temperature. It can stay in one form for a long time, or it can change shape very quickly. It is still just water, the things that make up water. This is similar to the body with a spirit housed in it. The spirit can flow and change and move.

When the body "dies," not all of the cells die at once, in an instant. Some body systems may stop, but cells continue to have energy and communication long after those systems shut down. Death appears to be a moment, but dying is a process. Death is but a milestone in that process. When a person is dying, before 'death' occurs, there are transformations occurring. In your father's process, this is happening very slowly.

As you know, there are gifts in a slower death, which is the family and community's opportunity. These spiritual opportunities are available to everyone who is around the dying person. We will refer to the dying person as the Transformation Maker. The Transformation Maker is doing their own work. This is not the business of those around them. The business of those around the Transformation Maker is to create a path to the Nest of the Dead.

The Nest of the Dead is not something that is easy to explain. This is because Westerners have very few concepts in place that will help you to understand it. The Nest is a 'place,' another set of coordinates in the Zone, where the spirit goes to await the cessation of cellular energy in the body. The spirit would like to travel on with as much energy as possible, with as much continuity as possible. This is why people who have died and come back report that they were somewhere nearby, watching events that were occurring around the body they left behind—their transformation was not complete.

And then I am thinking of how I saw my mother's spirit at her graveside. It was a collection of small lights that winked out one by one.

You witnessed the completion of her transformation. She was able to do this because she was able to rest while the transition occurred. You believe that you only witnessed this transformation, but you assisted her by bringing her along from the place of her death to the place of her resting.[35]

Now I am thinking of the many cultures that prescribe a certain amount of time between the moment of death and the burial, often four days.

This is ancient wisdom in practice. These days allow the dead to rest while their transformation is being completed.

A'riquea said that I could clear the path, remove obstacles, to the Nest of the Dead. What kind of obstacles?

There are things that can clutter the path to the Nest of the Dead. Anything that prevents the body from fully transforming.

I have puzzled many times about my father's pacemaker—a man-made machine that is forcing his heart to continue pumping. He could choose to stop eating or drinking if he really wanted to help himself die. There are things I could do to help him along, like offer sedatives, or a magnet for that pacemaker. I have not brought these up. It doesn't seem to be my place.

It is not.

[I am relieved.]

It is not your place because these are things that hurry the transformation process. It is true that he will go when he is ready, and that is not just a physical action.

Back to the obstacles.

The obstacles that lie in the path of transformation are Points. Points are places where the Transformation Maker gets attached, gets stuck.

Money seems to be one of my dad's attachments. He grew up in dire poverty but built a comfortable cushion during his lifetime. In his eyes, it is still something that defines him.

Money can be one of these obstacles, but once again you are stuck on definitions in the physical plane. This is not surprising, since most of the human world is centered on physical points. It would be more helpful to think of the energy behind these physical points. What is the deeper connection of any physical attachment?

There can be fear of letting go, of not having enough, issues

---

[35] My mother's process is described in *Traveling Light*, p. 17-20.

about independence, status, identity, recognition—the usual characters that prop up the ego. As you know, the more you focus on these, the more attached you become. What is required is a shift in attention. Not away from the attachment, because that continues the attachment by using it as a reference point. But a shift in attention to something else.

What is the something else? The something else is another dimension. It is what many people think of as Heaven. Heaven is just the place where the body does not follow. After resting in the Nest of the Dead and completing the non-physical transformation, the spirit travels on. The spirit is not free of the body, it is free to travel without it. Many beautiful things come with this travel. Humans tend to focus on the loss of the body, which is the loss of a certain kind of manifestation. Transformation allows another kind of manifestation.

Now you want to know what that other manifestation is. That is an entirely different conversation. Your directive to clear the path to the Nest of the Dead is to help your father feel *what he will be gaining by going there.*

Of course, I also want to ask what happens in the Nest of the Dead. Is this the reckoning that is sometimes described as the Pearly Gates? *This is not your business right now. You are to help clear the path.*

I decided that I would try to have a Last Talk with my dying father, not knowing if he would be alive the next time I saw him. I decided on the Four Statements format. This format uses four basic statements to help clear away old business and create a no-regrets goodbye. The statements are: I'm sorry, I forgive you, I love you, Goodbye. I approached my father and initiated this conversation. He was a male, born in 1929, and uncomfortable with deep emotional exchanges of almost any kind. Our Four Statements conversation lasted less than two minutes.

It was good for me to have made the four statements myself, but I had to let go of the idea that this was anything we were going to connect over. It was my agenda, not his. I needed to go back to Universal Wisdom's last point: Your directive to clear the path to the Nest of the Dead is to help your father *feel* what he will be gaining by going there.

When it was time for me to leave him briefly and travel to my home state for personal business, we hugged. Previously I had only hugged him while he was seated. His legs were weak and he was unable to get up and down out of a chair or stand up for very long. I helped him get up and we had a full body hug. I felt him in my arms, this once over-six-foot man, now small and feeble. His body was barely there. But our spirits joined in a few moments of warmth and complete energetic connection. In that surprising moment, I had touched on my directive to help him feel what it would be like to go to the spirit world. Going would be easy and comfortable and loving.

As a nurse I have worked with many dying patients. Some of them were, like my father, slowly exiting at home. Others were in the ambulance en route to the hospital and left suddenly. In either case, I was often aware of an ancestor waiting to greet them on the other side. The ancestor might have had a table set full of delicious food, standing at a door inviting the dying one in. Sometimes I was not physically with my clients when they passed but I knew the moment that they had gone, because I saw them pass through the door and take a seat at that table.

When my father passed, I looked up to the place near the ceiling where I had seen my mother before. Both the Spirit World and my mother were visible. The Spirit World appeared as a brilliant white cloud of lovely energy, gently bulging downward into the room. My mother had made a comfortable white bed in a beautiful white room for her husband. She was waiting for him to enter and rest. Everything was brilliant white. All of it was peaceful and welcoming.

After my father's last breath, my brother and I stayed with him and washed his body. Washing the body is a very old death ritual, typically done in earlier times by the family or community. In modern times it is often done by a funeral home. I felt that a ritual washing of his body was something I needed to do, even though I'd never done anything like that and didn't really know how. I decided to begin and let the process inform me as I went along.

I filled a basin with warm water. As the water was running it occurred to me that the temperature really didn't matter, since he probably wouldn't feel it. I made the water warm anyway. The use of soap felt harsh. I looked around in the kitchen and found some rose petal tea bags to steep in the water. I washed him with a soft cloth, starting with his head and working my way down to his feet.

I expressed gratitude for each body part as I went, speaking out loud. "Thank you, mouth, for all the wonderful flavors you have experienced, thank you for taking millions of breaths, thank you for helping dad's voice come through." Because we were at home, we had no interruptions and unlimited time. The process was loving and intentional. We moved from head to toe. When we were done all medical trappings had been removed and he was cradled in clean sheets.

By the end, I realized that this washing had served several purposes simultaneously. It was an expression of deep gratitude for life in general, it was an honoring of my father's lifetime, and it was also a positive bridge to letting go.

༄

The body and the spirit eventually separate, but after the passing there can still be opportunities as an energy form. My father came to me several months after he passed to clear up some old business. I woke up in the night and he was there. Still half asleep, I was fearful and unable to be present. I did not interact with him. A few days later, I entered a meditative state to see if I could regain that contact. He came right away, needing to talk, and the following conversation unfolded.

He has his head bowed. He is a younger version of himself. He appears a little nervous, brushing the inside of his nose with his thumb—a personal tic I have seen him engage in a million times. He clears his throat several times.

I tell him: Whatever you say, I want to receive it without judgment or reaction. It seems you want to speak and I certainly want to hear whatever you have to say. I have the feeling it is some kind of apology or statement that will help you move along in the spirit world. Receiving that would help me too, and all of our ancestors, clearing the line of energy. I'm going to stop talking now.

My Father: *Yes, well. I'm not very good at this stuff, this heart opening stuff. But I am coming from a place where I am a little stuck by my regrets. I've been told it would help to say the words of atonement. To put things right if I can.*

[This whole time, he is unable to look at me. I am trying to keep my gaze down, even though I find it intriguing to be able to witness the mannerisms of a person I thought I would never see again.]

Yes, well, that is how this works, I guess. You get to come back looking like someone that they will recognize. This is all quite interesting. I never imagined that there would be a world like this, like there are layers, and I can be me and something else, altogether.

I just don't know if I can do this.

Well, you don't have to. This is your choice. We can do it some other time.

Can we? [He looks at me hopefully.]

Of course we can. This is not about me. This is for you, it seems. I'm not here to force this, only to make the opportunity. I'm sorry that I reacted with fear the first time I saw you. Apparently I wasn't in a good place to be a receiver.

Hmm. A little information came to me just now, that maybe you want to write a letter instead of doing this face to face? I am aware that big emotion makes you uncomfortable. Do you know that feelings are just energy? Not like electricity, which could shock with its voltage. It's more like Life Force—it can be very powerful but also very healing. Maybe you are afraid that you don't have the right words to make the energy shift cleanly?

I don't know about all that. I have traveled to the Spirit World, some part of it, where I am free from my body but not the patterns I created while I was in my body. I guess it's one reason why you take care of stuff before you go.

I think you knew that before you left. I saw you thinking about it. But then your body was so tired and worn out and ready to be done, there was nothing left to create such a shift. Maybe that's why you get another opportunity when you are without your body?

That could be.

What if I ask you some questions and you decide if you want to answer them?

That could work.

I suddenly feel very humble and grateful that I could be in a position to help you with this transition. I bow before you.

[He looks a little disgusted with this display.]

Anyway. That's *my* part of this.

[He looks thoughtful.]

Okay. So who do you want to talk to?

Well, I wanted to talk to you.

And what is the general topic that this might come under?

That's what I'm not clear about.

Is it a feeling, or an action, or a thought?

It's probably an action.

Can you describe it to me?

[His fingers sweep across his mouth, followed by his palm, as if to keep the words from coming out.]

Let's go a different direction. What is it that you want to achieve by doing this, whatever it is?

I want to make sure that when I travel farther away, the people who need these words will have them.

So it's a gift.

[He lifts his eyebrows.] *I guess you could say that. That's a nicer way to say it. I was thinking of it as a burden. A burden that I'm dragging around and it just can't go with me to the lighter place.*

An apology can be a gift. It may not change everything that happened in the past, but it can change the future going forward.

For everyone. It can lighten everyone's load.
That is what I had in mind.
We could all use that.
[He looks a little more confident.]
Alright then. I'm going to tell a story. This is the story of a boy. The boy is me. I've talked a lot about my growing up, my boyhood. In those stories, I was trying to convey something that I don't think really came through. There was the hardship, of course. There was the uncertainty of my dad leaving [dying], of us moving back to the farm, all this time of not knowing where we would end up, not really having a home. I don't think I understood too much of that at the time. I didn't know anything else. It's just the way it was. It's just what we did.

I was little still, and I was working on the farm. My grandfather's farm. There were things I really liked about that. It was outdoors, the smell of the animals, the Life in those animals. The smell of the hay in the barn, the way the animals had their own arrangements with each other, how they got along. That warm milk in the metal pail. The comfort of my face against the side of the cow while we milked. The green in the fields, the smell of the tilled soil. The smell of the rain. My grandmother was a beacon of love. She really loved us boys. She was kind of a round person, and her lap and her hugs were soft and warm. There were good things about the farm.

And there were some not so good things. Things I learned to fear and avoid. My grandfather was a surly fellow. Grumpy and irritable. He did things to the animals that I didn't like. He cussed them and hit them. He did that to my grandmother too. My grandmother tried to take as much as she could, so that there would be less for my mother and us boys. I hated to see my grandmother taking that. We were all afraid of him. He just rambled around like a hornets' nest and we all tried to avoid him.

I was a boy. What did I know? I could escape out to the barn or the fields when that adult nightmare was happening in the house. And then it turned out that the barn was not safe after all. Some rough men lived there. They were traveling workers, people who needed jobs and worked for not much. They were dirty, and some of them were mean.

Some of them did awful things to us kids.
[I see a skinny guy with a broad hat, his face scrubby and dirty, his eyes white under that dark hat.]
Yeah. He was one of 'em.
[He's hesitating.] It's your story to tell. Or not.
I can see it. He has his dirty hand around your throat. Another hand where it shouldn't be.
I was so ashamed. I was so ashamed. My body did this fluid thing. I couldn't help it. How could I have liked that? I was scared out of my wits and just trying to live through it. I was so ashamed.
I'm so sorry that happened to you. It's wrong what that man did. Something like that happened to me, too. I think it's not that uncommon, but no one ever talked about it. It changed the way I saw myself. I thought I was a bad person because that happened to me. I stopped trusting people. I became afraid of everything.
I was afraid, and I was angry. I thought my grandfather should know what kind of person he had working there. When I tried to tell him, he blamed me for letting it happen. I got whipped. Things were never the same after that. They were worse. The whole world seemed like a nightmare. The fighting by the grown-ups in the house got worse. I was happy to go to school, because that meant I was somewhere else.

And then even that became a problem, because my mother had no money. Then we were living in town, and I thought that was because of me. I later learned that my younger brother had been hurt even worse, and my mother needed to get us out of there. Bless her heart, that woman took a lot in her life. She really loved us, and I was really sorry when I had to leave and go work on my own. She was all I had in the world. I tried to stand up straight and take it like a man. But I was really a boy. I lived my whole life after that not sure if I was still that boy, a boy pretending to be a man in a man's body. Your mother was my lifeline. She was a girl in a woman's body, and we made our way together.

There is so much more to this. I could go on. But this is the story I wanted to tell. No one knows this, this beginning of my life that formed everything else. You do the best with what you've got. Sometimes that's enough. Sometimes it falls short. I'd like to think that I did well by my family, by my children. Sometimes you fall short, and that is how it is, I guess.

I've been told it's not the circumstances of your life, exactly, because everyone gets something to deal with. I see that here. Life gets brought along into Death and then we have a chance to go over it again and make it right if we can. That's what I'm trying to do here. I'm bringing my story into focus and seeing it more clearly.

What I wanted to tell you the other day was that I treated you the only way I knew. I could say that it wasn't personal, except that you were my child. I understand so much more now that I'm here [in the Spirit World]. *I didn't see those things when I was there on Earth. I might have seen them, but they didn't fit what I thought things should be, so I let it go. I did a lot of blaming other people when I should have been looking at myself. There. That's what I needed to get around to. I was blaming other people for my own shortcomings. I took out my history on people who had nothing to do with that, because the people who were responsible for that were all gone from me.*

And what is it that you want to say to change that?

I'm sorry! [He's sobbing. I'm crying.] *I'm so sorry! I want to take it back, but I can't. It's too late. It's moved on through other people, into their lives, and I can't stop that.*

But we can change the energy of it. I can say thank you for sharing your story. Because it helps me understand you better. It helps me to not personalize it so much. I am going to say I'm sorry too. I'm sorry for reacting and creating disharmony. I'm not sorry for standing up for myself. It's what you tried to do too. It's what we all need to do. But then we also need to see the bigger picture. Who knows what made your grandfather so ornery? Who knows what made the farm worker overstep a child's boundaries? We are all connected. By our behavior. By our humanity.

I can be a bigger person. I can learn from this, and from my own life, and choose to live within a larger perspective. There is room for your history. There is room for my history. There is room for our history. Because there is room for everything.

I love you, Dad. I miss you. It was a mercy when your physical journey ended. I appreciate getting to be there during your dying process. I am very very grateful for the safety net that your life has provided me. Thank you for my life, for this person I am, with this physical presence on the planet. There are so many gifts here, and I am grateful to be given this opportunity. Thank you. You are welcome here any time. This is one of my gifts—being able to make contact in this way. I also know that you are on your own journey. I may see you again and I may not.
Call on me.
Thank you. Sometimes I feel very alone in the world. It is good to know you are there.
[I see him. He is with my mother, he has his arm around her shoulders and is looking at her lovingly.] You had a wonderful partnership. I'm glad you are together again. Someday maybe I will have this process with her, too. [She purses her lips together tightly.] Maybe not, haha.
Is there anything else today?
We have made the choices we made. That is called the Past. Being open in the Present, that is what makes the Future.

I learned many things from this conversation:

Personal history can be a source of pride and it can also be a burden. Either one of those create the points of attachment that obstruct our path. These points must be released in order to make transformation and freedom possible.

When we die, we leave our physical body behind but we take the energy pattern created by our living with us. We have many opportunities to clear these energies while we are in physical form. Apparently, there is also a chance to re-form that energy as we move through the next layers.

This is a clear example of the power of ownership, apology, and forgiveness. I can wish for a different outcome in my childhood, but focusing on that past is an ego function that traps me in Points of attachment. Seeing my father's behavior toward me in the larger context of his entire life, and the lives of those who came before him, helps release me from my ego attachments.

And, everyone has more to their life than I could ever know or understand. Maintaining that perspective allows us all to practice more loving kindness. Opening to a broader view of our lives and the relationships woven through it gives us an opportunity to heal. This can begin as
grief and loss and regret for things we might have done differently.

Grieving involves a deep sense of loss. A friend who was pained after his wife died told me, "This is a beautiful grief, because it shows how much I loved her." He felt that if his grief was less it would mean that he had not loved her well. Having this positive perspective or being able to accept death as part of life does not prevent us from grieving. Even when there has been much suffering and death is a mercy, it can still be hard on those left behind.

I was surprised to feel grief at my father's passing. I suppose I missed him. I'd spent so much time with him in his last year. Most of that was just being present while he slept or rested. Some of it, brief discussions about death and dying, was more intimate. There were a lot of personal growth experiences for me just from witnessing his process.

I think a lot about him waiting to die. I see him sitting in that recliner in his bedroom staring blankly out the window, as if there wasn't much to keep him here. He was ready to go and wanted to be on his way, but the trip was slow. He didn't have the tools to talk directly about it. He had a good death and I feel finished with that process. Then why am I sad?

Universal Wisdom: *You are feeling the effect of having lost something. It hardly matters what it is, although naming it sometimes helps you come to a place of clearing. What you may have lost here is some potential, something you imagined could have been. You may have wanted a better relationship with your parent, and it wasn't there. You may have imagined some deeper conversations, and they didn't occur.*

The time is past for those things to take place. Your grief is a form of regret.

There will always be that which is undone, incomplete. The ego will want to tell you that there can always be more. This is not true. There is only what there is. Your perspective of it can change, but the events themselves do not. What's done is done. What is undone is undone.

The done and the undone exist in the same space. That space is The Everything. Also in that space is everything imagined and not-imagined. Everything thought and not-thought. Everything felt and un-felt.

When your ego is doing the choosing, it will focus on either the done or the not-done. It is not capable of viewing both at the same time. That is the realm of Spirit—not just seeing, but holding, The Everything. In that realm there is no judgment, no regret. Come back to Spirit. Come back to The Everything. Let go of holding and controlling. Be. To find peace, practice Being.

༄

Someone once approached me, wondering if I could help them contact their mother who had passed on. I generally avoid this kind of channeling. The few times I have done it the ancestor expressed frustration at not being able to talk directly to their living relative. It's a like the old game of Telephone, where the message gets more and more garbled as it travels back and forth. It's also like getting in the middle of a family argument—it really would be better if everyone created their own lines of communication.

I agreed to get involved this time. The interaction with the ancestor occurred without the Earth person present. The Earth person wondered whether their mother had been "helped along" in their dying, and it turned out that there was not a black and white answer to this question about euthanasia.

A woman's spirit kept coming to visit. She was a well-dressed older woman, with her beautiful white hair professionally styled. Even though she had white hair, her eyebrows were dark. She was not very tall, and a little stout—solidly built. She reminded me of Barbara Bush.

Several times, she turned to face me and opened her mouth. I was to be swallowed into her energy. I hesitated, wondering if I should even be involved, but since she was inviting me I decided to just go ahead and see what she had to say.

D: *Well, there are a few things those boys don't know about each other. They were too far apart, as if I had two different families. And really, I did. Which was fine with me. But not with them. What is it about boys, that they have to be so competitive? I was exasperated, and I finally gave up. When they're adults, you know, they have to work out their own relationships.*
You look like a nice girl, maybe you understand what I'm talking about.
Yes, I think I do.
And their father, he was the same. Competing in everything he did. It's how we got where we did in life, but it was tiresome, too. I had to toughen up to be around all of that masculine energy, to try to hold my own. When my mind started going, I just had to give up on that, on that toughness. I became the soft person that I was before. And I had to trust other people, because I couldn't trust myself. That is a very difficult place to be in. The world became something bigger than I could manage. And, oh, all that money business. It was beyond me. I just did what my younger son told me.

If I had something to say about all of this, I would say that the money doesn't really matter, does it? It's just one more physical thing for you to fight each other for. Do you actually care about the money, or is it about who won? My youngest son thought he deserved it, after getting the short end of the stick in other matters. That's what he thought. And my older son, he wanted something else.
[She is looking away, thinking about this, about how to say it. Her hands are clasping and unclasping in front of her.]
I don't know just how to say this.
[Then she speaks to the son I know, the one who asked for this contact.]
You thought that your mother should be all yours, that somehow your

brother had no business coming in and claiming any part of me. I don't think it is something you would easily admit. And I have to say that I had some part in creating that. We had our little family, the three of us, and along came this baby and upset the apple cart. It took me a while to make the adjustment. I could've done things better. But really I did the best I could and that was that. I can wish it was different, but it wasn't. Your father wasn't much help, with any of it. I really was on my own. Oh, yes, my mother tried to be helpful, but I was having a hard enough time without her getting involved in it too. My mother was like me, and I didn't like that.
[She is a little distressed, going through memories I cannot see, and playing with a large diamond wedding ring on her left hand. Her nails are manicured and brightly painted. She resigns herself and lets her hands drop.]
Well, anyway. We can't change the past.
[She motions behind her and a man appears. He is balding, with longish wisps of grey side curls in front of his ears, and glasses with round lenses. He is in a suit and tie. He leans over so she can ask him something. Her head is turned behind her, and I can't hear what they are talking about. I think she is asking if she should tell something about her dying. Their conference over, he stands back, just visible in the shadows. She is seated, with her hands in her lap.]
Without looking up, she says, *I just don't know if it is helpful to say any more right now. I know that you would like to know, but I wonder why. How would you use this information?*

Because I did not die by my own hand. But I was an accomplice. You just can't imagine the situation we were in. By 'we,' I mean my son and I. There was no good solution. It would've been worse if we hadn't done it, if I had completely lost my mind and been unable to participate. Looking back, I'm not sure it was the right thing to do, but it is what we did. We managed to find someone who would help us. That is all I am going to say. We found someone to help us. He did.
In the moment of it, I was afraid. He should've stopped. It was too late then. I think that he knew he should have stopped, but he had his own interests in it by then, and it was not something he was going to give up.

I thought it was reasonable, until I was doing it. And then it was done. I am sorry I didn't tell you. It made for a messy ending. It just stirred up the competition between you two. I wish I hadn't done it. But who knows? Who knows anything? It's not for you to decide. Let it be.
[She waves her hand, signaling that we are done. She is somewhat distraught, crying quietly, and moves away.]
I am not sure what to do now.
[Her husband comes out of the shadows. He is angry and shaking his finger at me.] *Look what you have done!*
But I thought I was doing what she wanted. I thought she wanted to speak. This is exactly why I should not be involved in these family matters. It's not my business.
Universal Wisdom: *Do as she said. Let it be.*
So now I am carrying this, when it is not mine. Does it belong to me?
No.
This is how life is. It's messy. Just because I know this, it can't change the fact that it happened.
This is why I shouldn't be meddling in these kind of affairs.
There is always going to be some kind of doubt. Let go of this particular situation. It is not that important. You can be given many reasons to doubt. You will have to choose how to move forward.

The mother in the previous conversation chose to end her life rather than continue down the path of dementia. She wanted to control her body before her mental state prevented that. Anyone who has followed someone through the maze of dementia knows that it is a long and difficult journey. As the brain functions less and less it is unable to support bodily function. What happens spiritually during this cognitive decline? While my father faded away, I felt that he was spending more and more time in the Dream World, and that the Dream World was often present in his Physical World as well. There was some kind of bleed-through, or overlap. Is there anyone who would like to speak about this situation?

The Teachers are present and someone is getting pushed

forward, although she seems shy about speaking. She is a woman in her 20s with fair skin and short, dark hair. She looks like my mother in the 1950s—flared skirt and red lipstick, white anklets. I never had a close relationship with my mother, and I am struggling with my own judgments while trying to be open to her. She seats herself in front of me, fluffing her skirt before sitting. She is eager and ebullient.

Jeanie: *I have been waiting my turn to come.*
[Her hands are tucked under her thighs, her shoulders relaxed. She keeps looking back toward the other Teachers for encouragement.]
I want to talk about this because, you know, I went through this before I came here. I didn't really like that place I had to stay [the memory unit]. *I would have rather been in my own home. People seemed crazy in the care home. But we were all really in the same boat. Some were more crazy than others. I had my husband to help anchor me, but other people just went totally into this other space, because there was nothing to hold them back. I could still be somewhat in my Earth Life, even though I was moving towards the other situation.*

The day I died, it was so sudden, I was just minding my own business and then they [the ancestors] *came and got me. They came and I went. I was happy to see them because it seemed like a door just opened and I went right through it. Some of the other people on the ward had already gone through the door but their bodies were continuing on in the Earth World. Then there is a kind of disconnect. It's why you can't reach them, because they really are not there, not on the physical plane, with their minds.*

There isn't much you can do about that. It's not necessarily better to come back into the body anyway. It's just something you have to accept. That's hard for the family, I think, because they can't see the other world where their mother or father or whoever went to. They just know that their family member is not there.

It's a hard thing to watch. I went through that with my own mother [who died of Alzheimers]. *You just don't know what to do, because they're not there, but they are. You can't reach them. You don't have the usual feedback from caring for someone, which makes it feel futile.*

I guess you could think of that kind of caregiving like, "How would you want to have your house taken care of if you were away for a few years?" You're not coming back, ever, but the house is still standing there, with everything in it that you ever loved. That's your body. You try to dress them and feed them and keep them safe. That's maintenance. No one is thanking you or even enjoying what you're doing for them, because the spirit is away. Not 100%, but enough to make it difficult to respond.

Here is where body, mind, and spirit come together. The body is still going, the mind is not, and the spirit is around but traveling in other dimensions. It's a little like a sleep that you don't wake up from. Imagine you were living in your dreams. There is not much you can do with your body there. Sometimes people "wake up" briefly, from some kind of familiar sense like music or taste. But it will never be enough to keep them awake.

I think that the actual state is not so painful for the person with dementia. They have less and less awareness of the five sense world. But people around them in the five sense world have to deal with it. Whether you are the State, or the health care worker, or the family. And everyone has their own skills for managing it. This is a first world problem. A real problem, for sure, but it just didn't occur much in earlier times. People died of something else before they got old enough to lose brain function. Or if they did, they were cared for by family until some natural event (like illness) took their lives. Westerners are so afraid of death that they do anything to avoid it, even when death would be a mercy.

I'm not saying that there isn't some benefit to this whole situation. It gives Westerners a chance to examine their own spiritual lives, and their spiritual connection with their family member, and see how different people deal with things like this. It's all about learning, isn't it? It's about taking all of these experiences that you have, and not making sense out of them, but integrating them into your ability to see further.

That's what is needed—the ability to see further into the Universe. Not to get stuck in the five sense world and try to control *everything. But to let go and allow and see deeper.*

Flow. That makes me think of dancing. I loved dancing, even though I did not get to do it very much. Yes, it was hard when my legs quit working [from Parkinson's], *but by then my mind was deteriorating too and I just couldn't do it anyway. I just couldn't do much of anything. I liked being taken care of by my husband, I liked that attention. I did not like being taken care of in the nursing home, because those people didn't see me. Some did. But it was a bad existence and I'm glad I got to leave that.*

Do you have advice for people who are caring for family members?
Oh, I don't know. Comfort is nice, I suppose. Which means things that you recognize, if you can even recognize them. I would say just stop worrying about it so much and enjoy being with your family member. Have some parties. Have people around. Laugh. Don't be all grumpy about it. It's not like we can control it any more than you! We might as well be having a good time.

What are you doing when your body is in the five sense world and your spirit is somewhere else?

She leans in as if to tell me a secret, and whispers mischievously, *Well, wouldn't you like to know?!*

Haha. Of course I would, that's why I am asking.
That is not my area. You are going to have to ask someone else. I'm new here, you know.
And now I've gotta go.

She gets up and turns to wave to me as she leaves.
Buh bye!

I have to smile.

This information was interesting on many levels. To begin with, this was the first time my own mother had spoken to me after her death. Given our lack of emotional connection while she was alive, this conversation presented me with some challenges. Initially, I felt myself judging her. Judgment is an ego function and it is difficult to channel while focused there. I had to work a little harder than usual to let go, to let things Be.

Then, she presented as a young woman in her 20s, which I assume is how she prefers to be "seen." She was always quite concerned about her appearance and actively denied her age her whole life. She also had a perpetually innocent and sunny personality, which shone through in this exchange—giving me more appreciation for that quality in her.

I was a little surprised when she said, "I'm new here." She had passed on almost four years earlier, but she was apparently a novice. The other Teachers were there and she relied on them for support. Maybe there is some kind of training process. Of course, frames of Time in other dimensions do not necessarily line up with ours. An entire life on Earth could be just an eye blink, a little night out, in the life of Spirit.

I found it difficult to follow her at times. Maybe this is because she is a novice? Or because she had been both a person with dementia as well as a caregiver of one, and she was switching roles as she spoke? Regardless, that's how it came through, so that's how it's written.

Much of the information travels the thread of ego attachment. People with dementia are detaching from their physical identity. It's hard enough for them to understand who *they* are, let alone who everyone else is and how it all connects. We do best with them when we let go of our need to keep them confined in old structures. To let go, we also have to give up our identity of who *we* are, in relation to them. This is not easy, especially when we have developed lifetime roles and expectations.

Jeanie encouraged us to let go of specifics and put our energy into quality vibrations. She wants us to focus on fun, because the person with dementia can still relate to that feeling, regardless of who is producing it. Wouldn't you rather be somewhere where people are laughing and having a good time? It's uplifting!

Jeanie also encouraged us to use the opportunity to «*see further into the Universe. Not to get stuck in the five sense world and try to control everything. But to let go and allow and see deeper.*» That is the directive in almost all of the information from the Teachers—to let go, to allow, to see deeper. And then to use that experience to bring the resonance of harmony back into the physical world. No matter who we are with.

This discussion about dementia focused on giving up the ego connections of identity. That's something important to think about in our everyday lives. Why is everyone trying so hard to be ordinary, to be like everyone else? To have the right appearance, the right relationship status, the right friends? There is a very real biological function to belonging. It helps assure the survival of an individual and their gene pool. To that end, humans have been over-achievers. But constantly comparing ourselves and trying to measure up is a time-consuming waste of energy. The life we end up forming is full of people who share our anxieties, with everyone trying to console each other into feeling that we really are okay.

What is identity, anyway? Identity is a function of the ego. It's the me-first part of our personality that craves attention and reassurance. Cultural identity is based in childhood experiences. Most of us are well past our childhood years, yet we still hang on to these ideas about ourselves—about our appearance, our social circles, what we are allowed to believe.

Identity, however, is not a fixed state. It shifts over time as we accumulate more experiences. Spiritual identity is no different. We limit what we are willing to believe when we cling to what we were taught to believe or what others think. We sacrifice spiritual creativity and freedom on the altar of safety and stability.

The discussion of the dementia process described a loss of identity—a person with dementia eventually loses the awareness of who they are. Interacting with them works best when we are able to drop our expectations of who they are supposed to be and what our relationship with them entails. In other words, we have to let go of both their identity and ours. This is good spiritual practice in general—seeing each person as a spirit traveling the Earth and interacting with their energy in the present.

When we are able to let go of the safety of identity, we will open to new ideas and ways of being. It doesn't mean that we have to throw out who we think we are or where we came from, it means that we are willing to open the next door of awareness.

While dementia describes a gradual reduction of the identity attached to a body, there are other conditions which can expand our notions about an Earth identity. Someone I know had an organ transplant. They celebrate this new life annually, with part of the celebration including a meeting with the donor's family. Now *there* is an intriguing death experience!

I wondered about the person who died and donated all of their organs to dozens of other people, now living. If the spirit is resting in the Nest of the Dead, waiting for all of the body components to fully shut down, what happens when those body systems do *not* shut down? When they live on in other people? How can the surviving family members not be transformed by the awareness that their family member is still alive in multiple other people? Are the donor's family and the recipient now genetically related? So many questions!

The Library Man: *Ah. This is an interesting question. The spirit of the woman who died exists in every one of those organs. A kind of Twinning takes place, where the spirit of the donor and the spirit of the recipient share one body. Although this specific arrangement was not possible before medical science created the possibility, it has always been occurring through genetics. Genetic inheritance combines the information from many past lives and spiritual adventures. These can be expressed in the current body, improving or inhibiting adaptation to the current situation. It is a kind of partnership.*

Transplants are a kind of partnership also. Of course, the partnership is somewhat forced by the medications that keep the recipient body from killing off the donor's organs. But it is a partnership nonetheless, because without this arrangement neither the organ donor nor the recipient would have continued living. To be clear, we are talking not only about physical survival, but also spiritual continuation.

And now you are wondering about the donor herself, whose spirit has moved on without the energy of the donated organs. This is a new mutation in the human condition. It is one of the many reasons that humans have a specific niche in the Universe of Beings—here a new possibility has been created that has not existed before. People who donate one or several organs can move on. This is not a problem. Each organ has its own set of energy components, so there will be something missing when one of the organs is missing.

But a person who has donated all *of her organs is in another situation spiritually. There will be much information missing in the transfer to the next plane. It will be like Swiss cheese, where there are holes in the spiritual body. It may not be necessary to "fill" in the holes. It is possible that the spirit with openings is, as a new "model," open to new possibilities. This is the beauty of evolution—unpredictable changes with unknown potential.*

And what about other changes, such as cloning or genetically modified organisms?

Cloning is another kind of Twinning. The clones each have the potential to replicate the spiritual body from which they come. This may or may not be possible, depending on the particular spiritual body that was cloned. Genetically modified organisms also have this potential.

All of the changes have many potentials, for both improvement and debilitation. It is well to remember that no individual or group exists alone. Everything is dependent on everything. That is the arrangement. Changes made in one area will have effects in others, whether they are evidenced immediately or much later. It is not possible to predict what the effects will be, since everything is always changing, and the future is unknown.

☙

The future is unknown. We can't predict when the hour of our death will come. People in the cancer community know this: cancer doesn't make life uncertain, it just exposes the uncertainty that is already there. It's important to not only recognize this unknowing but to embrace it.

"We do not know where death awaits us: so let us wait for it everywhere. To practice death is to practice freedom. A man who has learned how to die has unlearned how to be a slave."
~*Montaigne*

There is a beautiful saying that explains this even more deeply: *I want to be today what I want to be when I go Home.* In other words, if I die today and go Home I want to be in the best state of spiritual readiness that I can be, and since I don't know when I am going to go Home, I need to live every day spiritually prepared. This is something that we are personally responsible for—no other person or relationship or organization can do it for us.

A'riquea: *Your spiritual path, your purpose, is very specific to you, to each person. People can share a path for some time, but they are still each on their own journey. It is important to maintain contact with your interior and exterior Universe, with the place where those energies join, and tend it like you would a garden. The more positive attention and tender care you provide, the more vibrant the path becomes.*

One of the dangers of relationships is that people become enmeshed in each other's journeys. They lose sight of their own path. As long as the relationship supports each person's journey, it is helpful. When it muddies the water, it is not. This takes conscious work on the part of both parties. Of course, people are more attentive, or more able, or more tuned in at various times in their lives. Things ebb and flow.

The overall trend in life needs to be toward not just personal growth, but also toward spiritual travel. Spiritual travel is different. It can include personal growth, or be an outcome of it. But spiritual travel itself describes a movement of energy. It is the kind of energy movement that enriches not only the human who is making the spirit-walking journey, but also other humans and sentient beings and non-sentient beings. It is the movement of God-energy, the vibration of everything that is and has been and could be. This is the true nature of purpose—to move the energy of God in the physical plane, using the amplifier of the physical body, for the betterment of all. You need to be able to see yourself in this context, and to apply whatever you learn to the bigger picture.

Most of humanity is currently operating in a too-small context. The very small context is ego, and the ego-driven life. The larger context is Spirit, and the spirit-fueled life. Much of this was discussed in the first book, it needs to be remembered. Earth is not the only dimension that you inhabit, it is not the only journey you are making. There are worlds upon worlds upon worlds, and they all intersect. When the intersection is harmonious, then there is an advance in God-energy. This is what is called evolution. In addition to physical evolution, there is also spiritual evolution.

Be mindful, not of promoting this evolution, but of embodying it through your own thoughts and actions. This is your purpose.

And, there is something else. The something else is the weaving. Do not allow yourself to believe that following your path is something that you do only as an individual. Each person is following their path, but doing it in such a way that there is an interweaving of the paths, of the journeys. There is a flow, created along this interweaving of the journeys, that magnifies the God-energy of each purposeful movement into a broader path. This is the path that was discussed earlier: there currently are few on this interwoven path. When many join their paths together, it will become a super highway, capable of supporting others with ease. This is the longer-term, even bigger-context, goal.

I need to ask about the concept of "longer-term." There is currently such a sense of impending doom, with political oppression and covid collapse and climate destruction. It is hard to imagine that there is much of a future left for humans on this planet.

Whether you have one hour, or one week, or one hundred years left on this planet, every spirit-fueled moment counts. Do not give in to negativity, for that will surely take you off your path. All of the things you have mentioned will be catalysts for change. The change will seem catastrophic compared to the world you currently know. But the change will lay the foundation for the new world yet to come. This does not concern you directly. It does concern your children and your grandchildren—the humans of the future. This is one reason to take the journey of spiritual evolution. Another is to prepare yourself for the time when you will leave the planet, whenever that may be. But it is also to apply your Life to the service of creating the interwoven journey of energy. Doing this will improve everything else—past, present, and future. It is bringing the All together into the One.

~ 6 ~

Dimensional Evolution

Through decades of channeling, it has become clear to me that the Teachers' messages are much more than words and visions. These transmissions also carry in their flow the vibrational essence of the greater energy domains which are their source. By expanding our awareness to include these vibrations, we can experience the transmissions with our whole mind and broader sense organs. This shift allows us to go beyond just thinking about expanded consciousness. It opens us up to energy alignments that make inter-dimensional movement possible.

Opening in this way is a process. It takes awareness and practice. As individuals and the human collective realign their energy structures to accommodate this process and its source, evolutionary change occurs.

Everything has an energy imprint. We come into the world carrying the energy of DNA coding as a blueprint. A matrix created by the events of living, a web of energy interaction, is built on that blueprint. The energy expression of each unique human being, then, is the result of DNA coding plus a lifetime of experiences. The expression of any culture, and of humanity as a whole, is the collective energy expression of all our matrixes combined.

The energy matrix of an individual or a collective can be reconfigured through changes in behavior. The underlying blueprint remains but what is built on it shifts. During an evolutionary change the blueprint itself is shifting. Like a Rolodex, evolution is constantly turning the card index to come up with new foundational blueprints that expand our capabilities.

The Women's Collective:[36] *Even though you occupy what seems like a concrete location, you can still rotate the blueprints to another configuration. And then you are the same, but not the same. This is The Shift. This is the shift that is occurring. The blueprints are rotating to another configuration. That is what occurs in evolution. A shift into another way of being. It necessarily affects physiology, and eventually anatomy too. But first there is a change in the energy configuration, the way energy moves and the structures that it moves through.*

This is where you need to prioritize your energy, but you also cannot leave behind the "places" where you are now. The Shift involves a gradual movement. It requires that you bring along what you are right now, because that is the "place" where evolution is going to occur. It is not suddenly going to materialize out of thin air. It is going to use the current arrangement as a foundation and manifest as a change in this model. It is a step-wise process. This is why it is important for you to participate in it, and not just wait for it to happen. You have to be investing energy in each step as it occurs. It is a building process. One thing cannot happen without the other.

Everything is as it should be. It can not be something else. It has to go through this process. Think about any kind of improvement you have made in your life. It is built on the actions you have chosen before you came to the change. It is additive. And, as we have discussed before, trauma can be the catalyst for this change. Sometimes things have to de-construct before they can be built on.[37]

Another Teacher once said: It's not that something is wrong, it's that something is different.

---

[36] This is a new voice, similar to Universal Wisdom, but decidedly feminine: *We are the sisters who have gone before, who have made the path that you walk. We are* **The Women's Collective***. We are the spirit of feminine energy.*

[37] Trauma as a change-maker is discussed in *Traveling Light*, p. 154-58.

Humans are attached to the physical world, which aids in physical survival. Over-attachment leads to the feeling of loss when something changes. It can be good when something falls away. It is likely that there was something unhelpful about the previous arrangement, or something that was in the way of growth.

I am thinking about how important it is to change, in terms of growing. If I was still an infant, or a toddler, or an adolescent, I would not be the elder that I am today. Something had to change all along on the path of aging. This is good. It's brought me to where I am now and it's a place I want to be. It's rich. A lifetime of learning and moving forward. With each shift I had to give up something in order to move to the next place on my Soul Path. Stagnation is not desirable. It can be hard to keep up with the changing!

This is adaptation. Sometimes the change is rapid or sudden or piles up on itself. It is all necessary. This is Living. This is Life Force in motion. It's how it works. Sometimes you don't see it, because you are so involved in the small vision instead of the bigger context. That is all it takes— stepping away and seeing it from a wider angle.

I've been thinking about how things look from different vantage points. The same thing looks different from three inches away, from three feet away, from three hundred feet, three hundred miles, three thousand miles, three thousand light years.

We can always make these adjustments in vision. It is important to make these ongoing changes in perspective. That is how you will avoid getting too tangled up in the ego's perspective.

I think of looking at the Earth from out in space and seeing the humans crawling around on the planet—it looks like total chaos.

It is, and it isn't. Everyone is doing their best with what they've got. Everyone is trying. This effort, collectively, is what is moving human evolution along. Everyone is adjusting to the changes, and the mass energy has a collective effect.

I and many people around me are dispirited by the damage created by masculine culture. We are destroying our environment and disrespecting many people through these activities.

Patriarchy as a structure has been in place for some time. It has been supported through culture and socialization. Those supports have begun to pull away. People are seeing the limits of this kind of behavior. It once had a helpful place, but it has grown past its ability to be useful now. It is a structure that is being broken down.

A new matrix is being built through the behavior of contemporary culture. Patriarchy feels threatened, and it is lashing out. This behavior is pushing even more people away from it. You see the balanced structure that includes the feminine forming now, there are more and more women gaining power and using it for good. Some mistakes will be made, of course. That is the nature of change.

But this is part of The Shift. Humans are seeing each other as needing one another, as needing to work together and recognizing the spirit in each other. This is the context where you will do your best work—bringing people together by bringing them back to their spiritual core. You are helping to build the foundation of The Next World. Understanding this foundation will help you to move forward with purpose and ease. You cannot be distracted by the triflings of the ego. Step into the Bigger Context, and see your place there. Fear not. All is well.

Note that the terms 'feminine' and 'masculine,' refer to two parts of a balanced whole, like Yin and Yang. They are not the same as 'female' and 'male,' which refer to identity. Feminine and masculine describe essence, or energy qualities. Masculine energy tends to be directed and linear, based in analysis and action. Feminine energy tends to be collective and spacious, based in inclusion and allowing. They both have benefits. Masculine energy has aided us in the development of tools and technology. Feminine energy has birthed every person on the planet and nurtured us as social beings.

Our current imbalance is a result of culture's worship of the masculine at the expense of the feminine. The Teachers would like us to address this imbalance. One place to begin is to reduce our reliance on thinking and practice sensing. We can *think* about the concept of Time, but what we really need to do is to *feel* it. We are often encouraged to be 'present,' to be 'present in the moment,' but what does that mean?

The Library Man is reaching up to start writing on the chalkboard, motioning for me to type as he speaks.

What I want to talk about today is something that we have not yet covered. It is all related, because everything is related. But I want to show you something. I want to show you something about how we get to this place.

Okay then. [He is thoughtfully considering the blackboard, chalky hand to his lips.] *Let us start with the present, since this is where we need to be.*

The present is something that exists, but not for very long. We talk about being in the present moment, and this is good. It is a good thing to be thinking about, to be experiencing. The trick is that the present moment is always moving, isn't it? You can be in the present moment and then it is instantly some other moment. It is constantly moving. And that means that our attention must constantly be moving. Or does it? We have to define what we mean by 'moment.' If we are looking at a moment—we can call it a second just to have some frame of reference. Let's say you want to be present in this one second. That second, that moment, is swiftly passing into the next one.

There is a Time-Space continuum, which is always moving. If you are focusing only on the Time element of this continuum, then you will never be able to catch up and stay focused, because Time is fleeting. The only way to stay in the present is to focus on the Space element of the continuum. Space is the place where Time occurs.

I am stopping to feel myself in Space. This is the beautiful sensation of expanding in transcendence. Maybe that is why it feels so good—because I have been freed from the constraints of Time.

Yes. But you cannot just exist in Space. Because Life follows the rules of the Time-Space Continuum. What you are feeling is more akin to balance. *So much of what humans have constructed for themselves involves cognition and linear thinking. Everything is bound up by Time, at the expense of our sensation of Space. True connection occurs when we honor the gift of Time within* the context of Space. *You are wondering what this looks like.*

I seem to be able to experience one or the other but not both at once.

Ah, but you do. You are just not recognizing it. Consider dreaming, for example. Here your physical body is at rest, and your energy has expanded outside of Time. Your mind is simultaneously functioning in that world along a parallel Time-Space continuum.

I am happy to inform you that there are many Time-Space continuums. You can be participating in several at once and not even be aware of it. There is not just one. They are nearly infinite. I say nearly, because there are some limits created by the physical body, but we do not need to concern ourselves with that just yet. It is important to acknowledge that there are many. Humans tend to think that there is just one, that is what they think of as the present, but even then it is being constrained by the imbalance of prioritizing Time.

So, the first step is to see that Time and Space require a balance of attention. This can be felt by focusing more on Space than on Time. The ultimate present moment is defined by being completely grounded and completely expanded, simultaneously. Next, you must be able to see that there is more than one Time-Space continuum. You practice this on a daily basis by transforming your awareness in different patterns, such as sleep and wakefulness, such as mental concentration and daydreaming. One must practice letting go of Time in order to experience this.

Experience is the way to understanding. Not just mental understanding, but physical as well. The sensations created in a not-Time experience reorder—reorganize—the energy of cells and body systems, of whole-body energy. This is what practicing meditation and other forms of transcendence do—they create a change in energy that reorganizes the Time-Space continuum in your body.

This is how you reconnect with the cosmos—by recreating, in your body, the Time-Space arrangements of the Universe. This is what you experience when you take in the night sky full of stars. What you see before you, expansive and full of Space, is the same as what is within you. This is traveling outward to go inward, just a different direction than the traveling inward to go outward, but it is the same path.

This is what we want humans to be doing. If you focus on the news, you will believe that no one is doing this, because it is not being reported in any way. What is on the news is all of the behavior that is not this. But it is actually occurring everywhere, in the private and personal and communal moments of living. This is the place to focus.

Understand that learning is a process. Don't worry about making mistakes or losing the thread. Just keep bringing yourself back. 'Practice' means repetition—in different times and spaces and arenas, with differing dynamics. It is all practice.

I have heard your mind asking throughout this discussion if there is another name for the Time-Space continuum. It may be called Life Force. It is what is informing every living thing on its journey. It is the energetic road map of the matrix. It is the Great Mystery. It is God. Time-Space Continuum is just the mathematical term.

The Library Man has asked us to recreate, with our bodies, the Time-Space arrangements of the Universe. This means that I will have to let go of what is called 'head-stuck-ness'—focusing exclusively on my intellect, on frontal and upper body energy. Similarly, I can also be stuck in the animal brain of emotional survival energy, or reactivity, which is ego.

Practicing transcendence brings my energy into all of my body. During transcendence, I especially notice an expansiveness in my belly and spine. With this arrangement I am more aware of the concurrent presence of multiple dimensions, dimensions that are co-existing in the same space where physical reality is taking place in my body. I'm more aware of their energy existence. I'm placing my attention there.

The Library Man is here again in his lab coat. He has his arms folded across his chest, with the fingers of his left hand absently touching his lips. He is very calm and thoughtful.

His energy feels very dense, vibrating more slowly than usual, as if we are in the thicker, gel-like, atmosphere of the Universe. He is speaking but it sounds like slow-motion and I cannot really understand it. Suddenly his voice and movements are very fast, like hyper-speed, and I cannot understand that, either. He approaches me and his face looms within inches of mine. He opens his mouth and swallows me. I travel down the dark chasm to become his energy body. Now it is his body that is sitting here doing the typing. He has manifested in my body. He is curious about my surroundings, the random details of my little one-room house. He is humored by a refrigerator magnet of Albert Einstein. *That's very good there*, he says, chuckling.

Now. I am going to be typing. And it is going to be just me. You are not going to be talking or asking anything, because this is far beyond your awareness. I can make more headway if I just write it, without having to explain it. So here we go.

So. There is a beginning to Time, believe it or not. There is a beginning to Time, and it is the thing that is the kernel of your Being. The beginning of Time. It is what was here before anything was here. This is a long way back, but it is held in the seed of your Being. This is the vibration from which all things come. It is not something you can ever understand, because humans are so bound up in Time. All of the ideas, all of the concepts that form human existence, have the edges of Time as their boundaries. It is part of what makes the human journey unique.

There are other realms which do not use Time to define reality. There are infinite numbers of other ways to describe dimensions. One of the reasons it is so difficult for most people to grasp the idea of multiple dimensions is because they are so attached to this idea of Time. Give it up, and you can go places.

You are thinking of Carlos Castaneda's journeys, and how he and his companions went on for long periods in other dimensions.[38] *This is exactly what I am referring to. Like being in a sleeping dream, where*

---

[38] During his life, Castaneda authored at least a dozen books about travel in other dimensions. One example is *The Art of Dreaming* (HarperCollins 1993). His work was sometimes discredited as 'fiction' because the existence of certain people in the books could not be verified. But the tools of science are crude compared to the vastness of the Universe. How could I possibly verify the existence of any of *my* Teachers?

everything is suspended that usually sets the limit of what can occur.

I want you to sit with this notion, of dimensions unbound by Time, and start to feel what that might be like. Focus on the sensation. Let your energy move into different alignments. Allow it. Feel it.

The Library Man speaks about the need to focus more on Space, not because Space is more important but because that focus may help to offset the anchor of Time. It creates more balance. There is an exercise that I find helpful for increasing my awareness of space. It involves looking for and finding space in smaller places and greater amounts all around me.

A good place to start is in the forest. Sit still and center yourself. Quietly notice all of the space above the trees. Notice the clouds, evolving formations of air and water. Recognize the space beyond the sky, which is the Universe and everything in it. Return your attention to the trees, and add all of the space between the trees to your awareness. Add the space between each twig on each tree, and all of the space between each of the leaves. Then recognize all of the space that is under the tree bark, between each blade of grass on the ground, between the hairs on the back of a buzzing fly. Keep adding. Really look. Become aware of all the space that exists everywhere. Keep looking and realize that there is much more space than matter.

In a city, stop and look above the buildings, look at all of the sky. Recognize the space between the buildings. Acknowledge the space in the rooms *in* the buildings, between the people on the street, between the cracks in the sidewalks, under a pebble, between your foot and the ground. Under your feet, open your awareness to include all the layers of earth and rock on the planet. Know that under your feet, if you keep going all the way through the Earth to the other side, there is more sky and an infinitude of stars. Allow all of that space to exist together at once and allow your awareness to rest there.

In your home, become aware of the space in all the rooms, under the table, under the chairs, under the bed, between the sheets on the bed, between the threads of fiber weaving the sheets together. On and on and on.

Keep expanding your awareness. Look at your own body and know that there is space between your clothes and your body, between each hair on your head, inside your nose, inside your lungs, inside each cell in your blood, between the atoms in the molecules in your blood.

Keep looking, becoming aware of more and more space. Gently hold all of that space at once and see that it is all connected. Let yourself sense this collective continuity and without limits.

༄

Time is a limit imposed by culture, communal living, and the need to keep everything in a predictable order that we can all relate to. Time means getting pressed down into Points, it creates tension. Not-Time means allowing myself to exist in Space. Going on retreat is a good way to remove the pressure of Time and focus on Space.

Creating an intentional retreat means that I purposely reduce outside interference. I stay away from news and social media and other external distractions. I allow internal dialogue. I ask, listen, and respond to my intuition—both physical and spiritual. This creates open space to be self-directed. Everything happens, or doesn't happen, according to intuition in the moment. What I choose to do and how I choose to do it has a more expansive quality.

It's the opposite of how I feel when I am running errands. Then, I feel like I am actually running, because I am trying to get many things done in a short time. The goal is doing, measured against a deadline of Time. I often get lured into believing that if I just get all these things done then I will have more time later, when what I really desire is the feeling of having more space right now.

What I feel when I'm on retreat, whether that's a day or a week or an hour or a minute, is flow. I feel more open and free, in touch and in sync with the movement of a greater energy. Like I am floating effortlessly in water, letting myself move along with the current of a lazy summer river. I'm in the flow, and I *am* the flow.

The Library Man: *This is a good place to be, to be feeling what it is like. It is important to have this feeling, even if it is fleeting, because each time you visit it you are creating an energy memory of a "place"* *you can come back to. The more you practice, the more you will exist in this state. It is desirable.*

I have often been accused of being a Dreamer, as if that is something negative. It is seen as a negative when the static state of Time is what is seen as reliable. But what if we thought about the Dreamer as being attached to the Dream State, the Dream World. This is where all of the great mystics lived. You simply cannot allow your life to be run by Time and still have access to creativity and new ideas and growth. If we are to evolve, we will need ever more people to release themselves from the burden of Time and enter this Time-less quality.

It does not mean that you check out from the world, isolating yourself in a cave. You may go there to connect with Not-Time, but then it is important to come out and share this experience, this learning, with those around you. To connect and reconnect with others. It is not something to be hoarded. It is something to be shared.

I hear you having a question.

I have been thinking about technology. I have noticed that when I don't hook into news or social media, then the flow is more easily accessible. It is worth stepping away from technology just to have these sensations. I can see how the activity of scrolling on my phone is distracting, but where I go when I do it is also problematic—I'm gone from the present moment and lost in some kind of removed cyberspace. Yet, we have this technology and it has permeated our lives. It seems that there might be some purpose to this which we are missing, or have not yet reached. Or is it just another form of mindlessness?

This is an interesting question, because every thing that has ever been developed by humans also has this shadow side to it, this unforeseen negative impact. How could we have ever known that attempting to explain the Universe in a theory would come around to the building of weapons of mass destruction? But then some of that same application has also been used to develop medical breakthroughs that save lives. It is not the idea that is positive or negative, it is the application of it.

And here we have the technology of social media, which is basically the ability to communicate over great distances. It is not the technology, but the application, that creates a positive or negative effect. Everyone has to decide for themselves, consciously, how they are going to use this. Of course, there are larger forces at work when whole societies embrace or reject certain applications. It is not your place to be too concerned with this, since you have little personal control over social norms. You can be an example. And you can encourage people to be aware of what they are choosing.

The best thing, in any case, is to experience the flow of the Universe in your being, regardless of what else you do with your life. If you are experiencing the flow of the Universe in your being, you will know what to choose or not choose, what to continue, what to leave behind. The flow will move you. This is where we would like you to be—in the flow, feeling the flow.

Ah—what is the flow? It is all of the Time that has ever been, that will ever be. It is everything. All of the energy of matter and between matter, all of the Space. It is the Space-Time Continuum. Life Force. It is all of the energy of living and being. It contains many dimensions, infinite dimensions, simultaneously. That is being in the moment, being present—allowing yourself to be energized by all of the unknown, the unseen, which exists.

You are practicing this right now. You cannot find it by looking for it, only by allowing it. Allow it. Join us.

I see a crowd of beings at a doorway, clapping and cheering me on. I have been to this door before. It is the entrance to The Next World. As I say that I move through it. I step through, feeling their hands on my back as if encouraging me onward. Then I am in the vastness of Space. It appears to be dark, but I see that each "star" is a celebration of light and sound and laughter—like a party. I feel exalted, empowered, enlightened. My head is thrown back and my heart in my chest leads me forward, soaring through the lightness of Space, unbound by Time. My whole body is alive and energized.

I am rolling into a ball and zooming along, rolling as I speed faster and faster and faster. I am like an atom in a vast arrangement of exploded matter. I am traveling in arcs and raceways and spirals and loops. My only purpose is the experience.

Now the crowd at the doorway is motioning for me to come back. They are laughing and chattering excitedly as I return through the door, their hands on my back again as they usher me through. Here I am in my room. I feel the thin layer of skin which contains my body, a body which has been energized and reorganized from the trip out of Time. The atmosphere, the world around this body meeting me at my skin, is light and free. It is communicating with the lightness of the night sky inside my skin. I am vibrating, pulsing with the beat of my heart.

This is the beautiful travel that occurs when I allow my energy to join the Time-Space arrangements of the Universe.

෴

Loosening my attachment to Time allows me to experience the realms of Space. There are many everyday examples of this altered awareness. One of my blog followers asked the Teachers a specific question: what is the difference between a vision and a premonition?

It seems to me that this depends on perspective. A vision is a story given, a view which helps us integrate a larger concept into our lives. I think of premonition as a kind of intuition. It's rather specific, and it may not come true because it involves the future, which is malleable by the myriad of choices possible between the premonition and the event—the input of multiple people and events in the interim.

This also made me think of deja vu, which is the perspective of looking back. In deja vu I have the feeling that I have been in a scene before, as if I have a memory of dreaming it. It seems that the feeling of deja vu, the shiver of recognition, is the realization that I am correctly traveling my path, since the past vision and the present are lining up. There are plenty of other past visions that I either don't remember or that don't line up with the present.

Premonition, vision, deja vu—is it all about viewpoint?

The Library Man: *This is a very interesting question. I would want to know why someone is asking this, because that would affect the way that I would answer. We do not have this piece of information. So I will continue in a general way.*

As you know, the past, present, and future, as well as other dimensions unrelated to Time, are all present in the same space. There is no real separation except in the linear minds of human beings. Time is continuous.

So what is being asked is, "How can I know which time frame I am in in any given moment?" You are correct that it is a matter of view, of perspective. But that implies that you have some control over the time frame you occupy. Most people do not have this control. It would be an extraordinary level of development to be able to shift at will. It requires much practice. Carlos Castaneda described events such as this.

But the average person is much invested in the here and now, the place where existence seems to be the most concrete. So these small ventures into other time frames appear to be subnormal. But they are worthwhile in terms of education. Because there you have a window into what it would be like to time travel. Humans are capable of this, which is also why these small events are possible in your consciousness.

These events are small openings into dimensions of other Time. When you feel or understand something intuitively, you are being fully in the Present. You are connecting with the energy filaments that are passing through you and providing information.[39] You are picking up that information. The more you listen to this and act on it, the better you will get at listening to and acting on these energies. The more you ignore them the more they fall into the background. It's about where you place your attention.

These other windows you are asking about also have to do with where you place your attention. It is possible to follow these energy filaments and discern where they are traveling. Where they have come from, where they are going. In the case of premonition, you have picked up where they are going in the nearby future. It is also possible to discern the longer-term future, but this is another skill. This is what "fortune-

---

[39] These energy filaments are like threads criss-crossing the Zone. They are created by the movement of light and energy traversing multiple Time-Space dimensions, and are accessible to us when we shift our focus beyond five-sense reality. This is discussed at length in *Traveling Light*, p. 26-42.

tellers" and seers may be doing.

When you are able to reach back and see where the energy has come from, then you are entering the realm of deja vu. It feels predictive because you are making an energy connection between the past and the present. You feel that you are connecting to events that were shown to you in dreams, often in sleeping dreams. And this would be true. Because while your body and mind are "sleeping," your spirit is traveling in other realms. That is its purpose. But it is still somewhat connected to you by your physical body, and you have the ability to process some of what the spirit is experiencing, so it will appear to you as a dream. It is good to be aware that your spirit is traveling and moving energy. This is the importance of the sleep state, and people who are short-changing this part of their lives are diminishing the benefits of spirit being connected to other realms.

Yes, well we have traveled over many ideas here. Suffice to say that there are many more layers to this. It is good to be paying attention, to where your energy is resting and where your energy is traveling, what intersections you are experiencing. It is also reasonable to invite this kind of awareness, because it can help you to understand the multi-dimensionality of the Universe, something that humans are in need of accepting. It is always about understanding the larger context of your existence. Not just understanding, but living a life that takes this into account. Things become petty and ego-centric without it.

The more I am trained in the concepts and sensations of Time-Space, the more I become aware of their presence in the many states of my existence. I even experience more agency—the direct freedom of choice—in my sleeping dreams. Sometimes I am as present there as I am in my waking life. In one of my sleeping dreams, I was at a checkout counter in a store. I was having a friendly conversation with the clerk and we were enjoying the casual banter of two people who didn't know each other but were connecting through social interaction. He laughed and I left smiling. I went out into the street, where it was getting dark and snow was falling. It was a warm Spring evening and the street was slushy. I was trying to cross the street and had to keep looking for cars in all directions. In the middle of the street, my five-sense reality began to bleed through. It appeared as small white spots that grew in size, and I remember thinking that my eyes were getting ready for planet Earth. Then I woke up.

What is remarkable about this sleeping dream is that it was not some far off movie I was observing. I was not only *in* the dream, but I was present enough to feel like myself and interact at a very present-moment level. I was actively choosing what to say and how to interact. In the past, before I had this much agency, I would have been aware of where I was and what was going on, maybe even what was being said, but would not have been so personally present in it. This time I was even aware of the shift in energy between being there and coming back.

What is it that I'm doing in these dreams? It is some other energy space but it's not that different from where I am right now. Is this how we travel in other dimensions?

The Library Man is here. My questions inspire a look of whimsy and Love on his face. His hand is absently twirling the chalk between his lips and the dust is landing on his face.

Yes, well. This is an interesting place you have come to. We were not really prepared for this, because it is farther along than the rest of the understanding. [He is pondering this, standing with his left arm folded across his waist, his right elbow resting on it and his chalky right hand stroking his mustache.] *I need to think on this a little, to bring it together.*

Okay then, let's try this. [He reaches the chalk up to the board, as he usually does when explaining theory.]

There is an intersection, a place where planes meet, an interstitial location if you will.

('Interstitial' means: of, forming, or occupying an intervening space, especially a very small one. It comes from the Latin to 'stand between.')

It is not so important to understand exactly what this place is, except that no two things ever actually touch each other. There is always subatomic space between the two things. It may not be seen by the naked eye, but it is there. So, there is also an intersection between planes, between dimensions, that consists of small amounts of Space. It is why they appear to be two different planes.

The crossing over involves a transfer across this interstitial space. The transfer may be more, or less, complete when it occurs. Sometimes almost everything crosses, sometimes less than that. The amount of transfer is what determines what may occur in the next plane. The more complete the transfer, the more agency will be felt in the other plane. The less transfer, the less agency.

As an example: when we first started coming to you, we were doing the crossing over and you were opening your mind to our energy. Now we are meeting in that interstitial space, and sometimes you are crossing over to see us. The more practice you have in crossing over, the more effective you will be in the next dimension.

My mind is flooding with more questions. How do I know the difference? It sounds like it is desirable for me to be effective in another dimension. What would I be doing with that?

Yes, well that is why this is a little ahead of the game here. You will know the difference because you will feel it. That is all I can say about that right now. And what is it that you are going to be doing in these other dimensions? That is also something that cannot be explained in the current context.

Suffice to say that this is desirable. It is something we would like to have happen. Once you see what it is, it will be something that you will want to have happen too.

I imagine that going there and coming back will help me to bring more positive energy to this dimension. It seems that there will also be some benefit to where I am going.

It is all about sharing and enriching each other. That is all I can say about it right now.

Is there something I can be practicing or doing to prepare?

You must continue on the path you have made, for yourself and for others. When you are traveling well, the next world will open. You will come to it naturally. You do not need to worry the details or focus on any outcome. You need to travel the path before you. It is the journey that will

bring you there—the journey. Be mindful and open to opportunities, the same way you are when you are traveling with us like you are right now. And then I get a little nervous. Nervous that it will be too big for me, that I will not be able to handle it, that it will change me in some way that I don't want. I have felt this before. This fear tells me I am on the growing edge. I know that when I trust, and allow it, the outcome will be beautiful and amazing and I will wonder why I would have been afraid of it. So this is a good sign. I am about to grow again. I will be shedding some skin—skin that I'm not even aware I am wearing right now. I will be reborn into new energy and beauty. This is all good. Thank you.
[He is smiling, his eyes crinkling at the corners, an impish grin spreading across his face, his hands rubbing together in anticipation. He turns away, waving his arms like a windmill, and disappears into the mist.]

As I experience more and more agency in my sleeping dreams, I'm not just an observer of weird objects or situations, I am actually a participant. I talk to people, make decisions, and feel my body moving. It's as if I am alive in that realm too.

I once dreamed that I was going see a film. I had gotten there late and I was confused about where to buy tickets. I ended up in a back hall where I could see the audience from the stage. All of the seats were taken and people were sitting up front on the floor. I saw one of my friends sitting there. I made my way back through the halls around to the entrance, at the back of the auditorium, only to be told that they were sold out and there were no tickets left. A lot of other people were there trying to get in too. I told the woman that I had a friend I was joining up front and began reaching for my money. She told me to go on in and don't worry about paying. I jostled my way through the crowd up to the front, physically aware of my body brushing up against many people as I tried to fit through small spaces in the crowd.

I finally got up to the front. I ended up too far to the front, standing right next to the screen where the movie was already showing. There was a lot of color on the screen, moving like psychedelic flowers. The scene shifted to one with people in it, and while I was standing there I walked right through that screen and into the movie. Next to me in the movie there was a man in a 1940s light brown suit, with a white shirt and a fedora. We were in the movie together. Then he walked past me, right out of the screen and into the theatre.

I woke up right then, marveling at the inter-mixing of dimensions that had just occurred. I was already in the dream world, and then I traveled into yet another dimension. It wasn't something I planned or worked at. It just happened.

The Women's Collective: *It would be easy to think that this kind of multi-dimensional travel is attainable by just thinking about it, by figuring it out. That is not what you are implying. But it's an important point to talk about, nonetheless. This kind of journeying is something that will be practiced many times before you can begin to understand what it means. First there will be the doing. A non-linear doing.*

You have experienced a glimpse of what could happen when this journey occurs, although nothing about your dream was very intentional. It is good that you have noticed. It would be good to learn about the energy state that creates such an opening.

I assume that this is what people think they are doing when they are on a drug-assisted trip. I have always thought that such a journey was limited by the effect of the drug in the body—once it's taken then the drug is controlling the outcome, not the person.

Yes, well, this is one way to experience the journey. But it only really works when one has a skilled guide. In Castaneda's books it is only implied, but they are traveling using natural therapeutic plants, and with the supervision of medicine people. This is not available or practical for the average person. It is possible to learn to journey like this without the use of the plants. And you are correct in thinking that this is what we are asking you to do. It takes longer to arrive at, but then the experience is ingrained into your metabolism and is easy to reach whenever you wish. Much like the spacial dimension of this meditative writing, which used to take a lot of practice but is now readily available, and in fact

does not require writing or practice at all.
Similar, but on a much greater scale.
How can I prepare to learn?
It is good to be away from the distractions of city life. Spend more and more time outside, especially with openings for unlimited free-association. Regular physical exertion is necessary to keep your physical presence grounded. Choose your social interactions wisely, and strive to focus there on spiritual connection and exploration. Pay attention to your bodily sensations. You are used to noting the challenges created by your brain injury as obstacles to accomplishment. Turn your thinking around to realize that these are just the changes you needed to be able to make the next journey.

It is important to be able to disorganize your thinking. As you know, disorganization leads to opportunity and creativity. Note the flow of energy in these disorganized states, follow the flow and see where you go. Let yourself be surprised and delighted. Open up to larger consciousness. Help yourself into the next world.
This is very helpful.
Know is that we are standing at the threshold of the next door. We will be welcoming you through. Then you will know us.
I feel a little fear of the unknown, which I know is the growing edge, and then I also know that I have the support of my Spirit Teachers. All is well.

༄

We are being asked to practice occupying interstitial space, and also allow it to occupy us. Of course I want to do this, but there are so many details required to function in the human-designed world! If I let that consume my energy I end up drowning in distractions.

The stream of stuff to attend to in the physical world is not going to go away. I can, however, shift my energy investment. I can recognize my boundaries and set priorities. I can reduce my focus on pushing agendas and outcomes. I can reorganize my energy to allow for change.

A'riquea: *You are used to being in charge, making things happen. It takes a lot of energy to be pushing against Time like that. It would be* *helpful to entertain a more fluid concept of Time. You consistently see yourself as working against deadlines. Some of those are real but many are self-imposed. This is an outgrowth of your learned independence. When you don't believe you can rely on other people, that you can rely only on yourself, then you naturally believe that you are the only one who can make things happen.*

While it is good to have passion and creative ideas and energy, and work to effect change in the world, it is not helpful to see yourself doing this in a bubble. Networking is, literally, web-making. So that when something is accomplished, it has the support of others to keep its energy in motion. You cannot do this all on your own.

We have talked about this before. You have to be willing to trust, not specifically the people involved, but the process. The process that occurs in the making of a new energy pathway.

As I've been told before, "Create an intention and let it move itself."
The process has energy outside of the realm of Time. It connects to other pathways that are not obvious to you. These other pathways need a chance to percolate, to integrate the energy of the new path into theirs.
I am seeing the looping threads of energy from other teachings.
Yes, the looping threads of energy between points. The looping threads— of action, of thought, of intention. The looping threads cross one another and the current of energy travels through these crossings, through the lengths of the loops, where they also cross and affect many other looping threads. This transfer of energy is nearly infinite, in many directions and in many realms over many time frames. There can be effects far away from the original cross-point, with energy traveling back again across the threads, communicating a similar vibration, a harmonic. Sometimes this may be instantaneous. But it would not be helpful to expect this.

So there is a patience required. Planting the seeds, and then watering and tending them, but trusting the plants to know how to grow and giving them the opportunity to do this.
To every thing there is a season…
It is important to keep planting seeds. And to keep tending the plants. And to know when to harvest. These are processes that are working on a

Universal level, and cannot be controlled by your agenda.
Just like this channeled writing.
Similar, in that you need to zero out your own agenda, and make use of your energy by being open to that which comes to you.
And I have been using a lot of energy trying to control it all. This is a misuse of my resources.
It is a mis-direction of your resources. Look at what is draining you, look at what is frustrating you, and try to see how you could be working differently, how you could be letting go and letting the process work itself rather than trying to force it.
Consider more ease?
There is a time for action. There is a time for patience. There is a time for ease. Learning how to apply each of these will help you use your resources more effectively. Above all, enjoy your life. If you are not enjoying your life, appreciating it and feeling enriched by what you do, then something is out of balance and it would be worthwhile to reposition your energy.

I was given a lesson in this repositioning of my energy in the following vision:

      I see a woman in an office building and understand that she will be a business connection for me at some point in the future. She has short curly hair. She is wearing a reddish short-sleeve dress with small buttons down the front. She is floating above me with her head thrown back, her chest at my face and the buttons rubbing gently against my skin. I let this pass through me and then I am inside her ribcage. It is warm and meaty in there. I can hear her breathing. She is laughing at the silliness of this. She exits, turns around, and her body joins mine. We become one. Now I am wearing the reddish dress. She will be typing through me.
I am a busy woman. I run a busy office. We have a lot going on here. I want to tell you something about how this works.
She points across the desk, out the window of the office building. We are in a big city where the buildings are close together. I can see into the next building, one floor down, where a person is sitting on the window sill. The business woman keeps pointing at this other

person so I go over to the window and look.

The person is sitting in the corner of the window. It is another woman, and she is sitting alone. She is wearing a creamy gauze peasant top, and has a long dark braid that she is curling around and around her fingers. It is a slow, meditative, relaxing process. She is thinking. She turns toward me and beckons me closer. When I am near, she opens her mouth and swallows me. I am tumbling down, down, somersaulting as I go.

I am resting in her body. Together we are looking out the window toward the office building. She sees the business woman and waves to her. The business woman waves back. Then I also become the business woman, waving back at the braided woman. I am both of them, and we are simultaneously waving at each other. I can bridge this gap by existing in the energy that is between them, in the air between the buildings. They are waving. I am both of them, waving, and I am the space in-between them.

The energy moving from the business woman to the braided woman travels along one side of my body, while the energy from the braided woman to the business woman travels along the other side. The energy coming from each woman goes to the other. The energy is moving in opposite directions as it passes through me, creating a spinning movement. It spins me counter-clockwise. In the spin, some of the energy coming from each woman also ends up going back to her in the flow. They are waving and I am spinning. A connection is being made as I spin. My spinning in the middle creates an energy fulcrum.

I have been observing this. When I try to let myself feel it, there is resistance. My body wants to spin the other way. When I help it to go the other direction, clockwise, I feel a freeing. It is my own energy unspooling. My energy moves out into the Universe, both up into the sky and also down into the Earth. The unspooling looks like a gentle funnel cloud. It is a wonderful feeling of flow. All of the cells in my body have more space. There is more space between everything and this is a good feeling. A renewing feeling. A joyous feeling. My body stretches out and occupies more Space.

When I try to reverse the spin, I feel my energy crushing down, smaller and smaller. This is uncomfortable, deadening, irritating. I am like a coiled spring. When I am compressed by the "negative" direction, there is tension. When I am allowed to loosen up, it feels like laughter. The axis points for this spinning are the top of my head and the bottom of my feet. Being stretched out and relaxed allows the spring to vibrate freely. This feeling is where I want to place my attention. I will know I am in the Zone when I feel this feeling. It is a balance.

It is tempting to describe this in simple psychoanalytic terms, like the business woman is my left brain and the braided woman is my right brain. This disrupts the vision. The business woman has her head in her hands, exasperated with this intellectualizing. The braided woman leaves the window sill to go inside. I ask them to try again. The business woman indicates that I already had it. The lesson is the unspooling, the relaxed spring. There is no need for further explanation.

I am very tired. I think I want to leave, but the business woman is motioning for me to come back to her. I am in the office again. She is straightening a paper pile by tapping the edge of it against the desktop. She places it on the desk and smoothes the top page with her hand.

I want you to know about this. When you come to this office again you will need this skill. You will need this skill to determine a choice. Practice. It won't be long now.

[She puts the paper pile into a drawer and closes it. She folds her hands on the desk and looks up at me, smiling.]

You'll do fine. It's just another one of those tests that makes your skill evident to others. Not to worry.

[Now she is looking away and shooing me along.]

Loosen the Coil.

It seems that these two women were present in different energy dimensions. The business woman was in the Physical World and the braided woman in the Dream World. I was able to travel back and forth between these two worlds. I was also able to occupy and energize the space between them, which included both, by 'loosening the coil' —by opening my energy into a spiral to allow more Space and vibration.

Another vision explained the coil further. I dreamt that I was high in the air, on a tall ladder, attending to spiritual smoke that was rising from something burning below. I was up in the smoke and my position was very precarious, even dangerous. The ladder was not stabilized on the ground and I was tipping. I was up in the air with nothing to hold that would steady me and I was trying to balance by extending one leg outward. Standing high on a ladder on only one leg made me even less stabile. It was clear that I had extended myself beyond my spiritual skill level. I needed to be more grounded. **A Native Elder** was there, and held the ladder still while I climbed down. He said, *You have to know why you are calling the spirits.*

Now down from the ladder, I went to work maintaining the coils that created the smoke. These coils were like the incense spirals that are burned to repel mosquitoes in the yard, only much bigger. The coils were thick, as thick as my arm, and dark grey-green. They were wrapped flat spirals about the size of a trash-can lid, lined up in a row touching each other. There were five of them. I'm not exactly sure what the coil is, but it is related to the directive to 'Loosen the Coil.' Who can help with this?

It seems that you would like to elevate yourself to some kind of spiritual master. You would do well to wait and follow the path you are on. You are also a Teacher, and there are many ways for you to use your talents.

The smoke does not need tending. These are the prayers that have already been lifted beyond this plane. What needs tending are the coils, the source of these prayers. The incense must be kept burning for the smoke to rise to the level of the Spirit World. That is what is happening in this dimension—creating the prayers in the coils and releasing them. Of course, this is metaphor.

I sense that this is a lesson about multiple dimensions. The incense

is a compacted solid, but any compacted substance also includes air space within it—that's why it burns so well. Formed into a spiral, the coil maintains a circular path as it burns. The burning solid disperses its substance in lighter particles carried by the air. This smoke travels upward. It is most concentrated at the source and then there is more and more space within it as it drifts upward. The incense is the seemingly solid nature of the physical world. The smoke travels into the spacial domains of the spiritual world. The burning fire is the ignition of the two together.
This is why you will need to maintain the coils.
I assume the coils are within me. In the dream, the coils appeared to be outside me.
The coils are everywhere. Any place that energy moves, there are coils.
I see my own energy moving in a circular pattern, but it is not totally inside or outside my body. There is a coil swinging in my pelvis, like a pendulum. It doesn't settle, it just keeps moving.

  I am wondering about my low energy (a side effect of cancer treatment). I think I should do more every day but I feel so tired. I have trouble getting going, and when I do get going I often pay the next day with even lower energy. Is there something I am missing?
You are dancing around the energy question, trying to define it, when really it will be different from day to day. There are many factors. Spiritual, emotional, physical, mental. Some of this is a result of the treatment, some is your new lifestyle manifesting. It is important to be present. Understand what you are choosing.
I would like to know what creates the fire, the burning?
Praying.
Praying in the religious sense often means asking for something, but I think of praying as expressing gratitude and setting intentions.
Praying is something that is done with the heart, not the head. It is also done with the pelvis. It is about creating energy ripples, generating energy with intention. It is an action.

☙

We have traveled through some interesting metaphysical material so far. We've been encouraged to open up, not just to the words and ideas carried in the Teachers' transmissions, but to their vibrations. These vibrations arise from Time-Space continuums beyond our own. They can be accessed by reducing our focus on the limits of Time and practicing the expansive sensations of Space. When we experience multi-directional movement in other Time-Space continuums, we are supporting the current Shift in human spiritual evolution.

The Library Man appears peaceful and relaxed, and slightly amused at my attempts to explain: *Yes, well this is an important point, and we have been waiting for you to get to it, so here we are. This is the next part of the journey, the next leg, if you will. We have been discussing, for some time, the information and the need to align it with your daily life, the need to bring it into living. It is Life Force.*

But this next leg has to do with what is going to happen when you are able to move it along. Flow. Yes, this is about flow. There is a flow in the Universe. It is everywhere. It is often taken for granted in the physical world. No one really stops to think how much flow is going on every second. [He is reaching high on the blackboard with his chalk. When I report that, he stops and looks at me with an amused smile, as if to say, "Really?" Too much reporting.]

This is not going to go anywhere if you are focused on being the reporter, because that is an ego function—getting it down and getting it right and thinking about how it will sound. You are not the reporter, you are the recorder. That is how this works.

So now, we will begin again. [He points to the keyboard and then turns to the blackboard.]

There is constant flow in the Universe. Think of nerves, for example. Energy is always moving along these nerves, sending information back and forth, back and forth. The reason you are able to type this, the reason someone is able to read this, the reason anyone understands what is being said, the reason there is an idea to be discussed—it is all happening with the flow of energy.

We can break this down into molecules and atoms and electrons and such. What you need to see is that within any of these structures there is much more space than matter. The matter holds the energy, but the space is where the energy moves. It moves between the matter. It is not important how big or small the matter is, there is space all around it and space within it and all of that space is continuous. What we have been asking you to do is experience that space. You must have the imprint of that space in your cells, in your being. When you are comfortable in this endlessly-connected space, when it is part of you and you are part of it and there is no separation, then it is possible to begin moving in that space.

Let us see where this goes now.
[He is holding a mobile of the solar system, a model with planets drifting around on strings.]
This is the example, this model of your solar system. What if you are one of these solar systems. [I am feeling the sun in my chest, and the planets orbiting around in my body are organs.]
[He takes the model and wads it up in a ball, with the strings all tangled and mashed together.] *This is your energy in physical form. It has limited movement because it is connected by the strings, the precondition of the arrangement, the idea that someone is holding the model and the strings, someone like a religious figure who controls everything.* [He tosses the model away.] *That is crazy-thinking. The balls in the model are made only of styrofoam.* [He steps on one to show me how easily it is crushed, and I find myself feeling a little shocked and disappointed at this destruction.] *Throw away that thinking. I have done this on purpose, to make you see how fragile this thought construct is. It has no basis in dimensional reality.*

3-D is the physical reality where you are used to functioning. It describes the confluence of three axes or planes (like a grid using x, y, and z) to locate a Point. This is one way to define the Point, but it is a limited one. When you are limited to three dimensions, that is limiting your function to the physical plane only. That is what is meant by being stuck in ego, because it disallows other references that allow for expansion.

Adding the fourth dimension of Location means that this Point, this point defined by 3D, becomes located in Space. Say I have an object, let's choose the example of a fixed object to begin with. There is a table here. [He points to the lab table, touches his index finger to it.] *It is a solid object, as defined by physical reality. But right here, right where my finger is touching the table, is a location in Space. It is the interface between the table and my fingertip. I can touch the table, I feel it with my finger. We can look into the table top and see that it is made of a substance that is resistant to water and wear and heat and the general abuse that scientists dish out. It is strong and sturdy. If we were to look at it under a microscope, we would see that it is made of molecules and atoms and atomic and subatomic particles and on and on into the infinity of the micro scale. Infinite. Endless. It never stops going.*

We can also see that this table top is part of a table, which is resting on the floor, which is in a building, that is held by gravity onto the planet, and the planet is a giant sphere that is spinning around and around and around its axis, and it is also circling around and around and around the sun, surrounded by the other planets, who are also spinning and creating energy, and the whole solar system is moving through space, a little tiny speck in the Milky Way, which is itself a little tiny speck in the whole un-mappable Universe, the infinity of the macro scale. Infinite. Endless. It never stops going.

So you see, this table is a physical object that is one tiny tiny tiny location in Space. It exists on the continuum of endless endless endless infinite space. The fact that we fixate on it as a table is a function of our perception of physical reality. It also exists simultaneously in all of those other locations, from subatomic to galactic, but we choose to focus our attention on this one minute part of its existence, calling it a table. Those other places that it is located do not cease to exist, we just choose not to acknowledge them. We have to limit this, in order to manage all of the parts of physical reality at once. But all of those locations are also there. All the time. We can choose to see them.

Not only are we used to fixing physical reality based on Point plus location, we also choose to fix reality based on Time. And that brings us to the fifth dimension, which is also part of this table. I can place my finger on this table and see that it is a location. But it is also defined by Time. Right this minute, my finger is resting on something we call a table, in this room, in this building. What was in this same location twenty years ago, before this building was built? What was in this location 100 years ago, or 1,000 years ago, or 1 million years ago? What existed in this space trillions of years ago, or before the Earth was even created? What will exist in this location 100 years from now, when this table has been long gone, or 500 years from now, when this building will not even be here? What about a million years from now? The past and the present and the future are all a continuum, like a long long long string, without a beginning or an end, and everything on it is connected to each other along that string. It shares energy and knowledge and creation and death and movement.

All of these dimensions—Point, Location, Time—are constantly in motion, energetically, and constantly interacting with each other. This is the resonance you feel when a Teacher comes from another location or time to energize the Point where you exist. Your energy is enriched by contact with these greater energies, by the awareness of this expanded Space. This is the resonance that is vibrating in their words and ideas. This is what you feel when you practice transcendence, when you bring your awareness to all that has been, and all that is, and all that is possible, all at once.

This is what is being asked of you. In the first book, we encouraged you to let go of the limits of the ego, of five-sense-only living. In the second book, we encouraged you to open up to the addition of Spirit, the beauty and joy of including Spirit in the physical world. In this third book, we are asking you to expand into the Everything, to bring all of these dimensions into your awareness. Let the traveling begin!

He is looking to me with Love and invitation. He wants me to come into this world he has described, and that I feel in this moment. He turns to move ahead and waves for me to go with him. I skip up to his side and put my hand in his cool, chalk-dusted hand. He is smiling, and sweeping his other hand along the sky before us. He has been waiting for me to take this journey. I am ready. He turns to me, happy, and takes my face in both his hands, giving me a quick brotherly peck on the lips. Then he turns away and somersaults away into thin air. I wave goodbye. See You Later.

∽

This next section is quite complex—you may want to read it aloud for greater comprehension.

We have been talking about the energy structures of dimensions beyond the five senses. This is not just a concept to think about and understand. It is something we are being encouraged to actively feel and practice. It is the gateway to The Next World, and crossing this threshold is the change in consciousness that has been described as The Shift—the evolution of consciousness into another layer of being. I was thinking about this when I received the directive to "embody multi-dimensional positive energy."
The Library Man: *Tell me what you are already thinking about this.*
Well, 'Embody' means to express energy with the body, or through the body, which likely refers to transcendence.
'Multi-dimensional' means that it is occurring simultaneously in many Time-Space dimensions, including 'this' dimension of physical existence. That's another reference to transcendence.
'Positive.' You have talked before about the relativity of 'positive' and 'negative,' that everything occurs on a continuum, relative to everything else. I'm guessing that this has something to do with resonance, with how something harmonizes with other things or elevates energy. I'm feeling a little extended here, beyond what I really understand.
'Energy.' I don't have any way to explain that except to say 'vibrational movement.'
[He is listening, standing with his arms folded, fingering his thick white mustache. I see a formula that starts with x squared plus something. He looks at me with surprise.]
Yes, well that is my thinking process, trying to discern the mathematical description. It has nothing to do with you.
[He unfolds his arms and looks seriously at me. He rummages in the pockets of his lab coat for a piece of chalk and turns toward a

wall-sized chalkboard. He is moving the chalk on the board and as he writes little bits of dust are drifting down. He stops and leans on the chalk rail, turning to me.]
There is something about this that is not quite regular. I don't know how to explain this outside the mathematics. [He goes back to writing on the board.] *I will be writing in numbers, and you will be writing in words. Let us see how this can work.*

Alright then. When we bring the sum, which is really the sum of everything, around to the beginning of the equation, we can see it from a different point of view. Then we can see it from the way that it has been built, rather than the way it functions. These two things are well-related, but they are not the same.

He has a very complicated equation going. To simplify, I will just write it as $(x + y) = z$. This equation shows that when two things have been added together, they make something else. He calls this arrangement 'structure,' or how something is made. He demonstrates the change he is talking about by shifting the location of the parts, by moving the sum to the beginning of the equation, which then looks like $z = (x + y)$. It's the same equation in a different arrangement. This arrangement shows how one thing can be broken down into its parts. He calls this 'function,' or how something works. So we have structure in $(x + y) = z$, and we have function in $z = (x + y)$.

In order for something to function, it has to be made. But it does not have to function once it is made. There is structure, and there is function. There is also beauty, which is an equation that describes the relationship between these two. Today, we are only concerned with structure and with function.

Structure is also a function, because the creation of the structure is also a process, although this process is limited to the creation. Once the structure is there, it can be used in multiple ways, and so there may be more than one equation to describe the function of any given structure.

This is true with humans. A process created the structure, which is the body, the physical evidence of existence. The process of creation never really ends, but it does come to a point where there are fewer miracles. Yes, it is all a miracle, but the miracle becomes related to the function. For there are so many ways that the structure can be made to function.

For example, when you were recently looking at the duality of Grit versus Sensitivity as an outlook or a lifestyle—the hard edges of living and the soft edges of living. These are two different ways that the human structure can interact with its physical world. Two different functions.

As you noted, there is a larger context in which both of these are included. It takes a broader vision, a bigger equation, a larger energy, to carry both of these not only simultaneously but also as part of another structure, another function.

This is getting confusing, I see, but please bear with me.

So there is this larger structure which includes both of the dual structures. It is a structure of energy. It is the energy that is the glue between dimensions. And that glue is Space.

Space is an energy on its own terms. It is not just "empty," it is not just the absence of something else. It is a Something which includes Everything. Everything. When you are referring to The One With All, this is what you are referring to—Space. Space is around everything and in everything. Yes, if it includes Everything, then it must also include Nothing. That is another discussion. Let us come back to multiple dimensions.

I am stopping to experience this expansion. I am very tired, making it is easy to be half in the dream state as well as being physically present and also receiving the information, the teaching.

So then you are touching possibly three dimensional planes.

Imagine, if you will, that there are infinite numbers of dimensional planes. Yes, it is beyond your ability to sense or imagine. But accept for a moment that such infinity exists. All of those planes (and, of course, they are not planes, as in flat dimensions; it would be better to call them dimensions, because that implies multiple planes simultaneously within any dimension), all of those dimensions have energy moving within them, through them, around them. We are back to Space.

Space is the connection between multiple dimensions. Multiple dimensions, infinite dimensions, can be occupying the same space, and each of those dimensions can be contributing energy to the space. If you were able to access the positive energy of all of these dimensions, or even some of them, you would be pulling in great amounts of productive energy, energy that could be applied in this physical dimension.

Ah, and you are asking what happens to the dimensions which the energy is being taken from, do they become depleted? But energy is always available. It is only the form which changes, which is transformed when it crosses dimensions. When we are asking you to embody multi-dimensional positive energy (and that is exactly what you are being asked to do), the configuration will be a concentration of positive energy.

You have some experience with this already. Think about your interactions on your recent road trip. Much of what was most satisfying to you was the movement of positive energy, was it not? That is the beginning of the process. You have experience in the movement of energy. You know what it feels like. You are being asked to create a structure whose purpose is this movement of energy. Once the structure is in place, its function will follow.

I immediately felt a little rebellion, as if I was being asked to create a religious structure. But of course it would be a spiritual structure. Can you help me understand what this is?

You are thinking of this too literally. What we are asking is for you to be a site of energy concentration.

I have to ask if this is something that my physical body can withstand, being in the easily-fatigued state of chemo damage. Maybe concentrating this multi-dimensional positive energy will also have a healing effect on me? Oh. *Learning* how to concentrate this energy will have a healing effect.

Yes.

Because I am not just being asked to concentrate it, I am being asked to *embody* it. Embody—the dictionary lists 'embody' as an action: to be an expression of or give a tangible or visible form to an idea, quality, or feeling; to provide a spirit with a physical form. "To provide a spirit with a physical form"!

But I've gotten a little freaked out now. Am I being asked to channel a specific spirit?

No. Once again you are taking things too literally.
Sigh.
We will take a break and come back to this another time. Until then, keep the directive in mind.
Embody Multi-Dimensional Positive Energy.
Thank you so much for persisting with me.
Of course. Rest now.

We are being asked to develop a new skill. Not just transcendence but Transcendence Plus—allowing our physical presence to move the energy of the space shared by multiple dimensions.

Re-reading the previous teaching, I can feel my energy state condensing and expanding, transcending, rearranging, realigning. I have to curb my consideration of the propane repair person coming in the middle of this. It is no reason to delay. Thinking about it pulls me out of energy integration (that is a lesson in itself).
The Library Man is at the wall-sized chalkboard. He is still puzzled. He has been working away while I was resting. I will wait patiently. It is a chance to practice being in this beautiful state.
Yes, well, we will continue and see where we can go again.
Let yourself relax with the idea that the repair person may show up. He is also a scientist of sorts, working with energy and matter.
   So. We were talking about the concentration of energy, positive energy, from multiple dimensions simultaneously. This is the work you are going to do. You cannot imagine it right now, because it is not something you physically know yet. It will come in time. I am in your body today because it is important to have the sensation that comes with this concentration.
[Now I have his wild white hair, his lab coat, his thickish hands coated in chalk dust.]
It is not just concentration, but movement. The movement is critical. Concentration is what will build the structure, but movement is the desired function. It is not going to be some giant display of fireworks,

like you are thinking. It will be using every cell, and every space in your body, to perfect attunement. I am intentionally using that word because it brings to mind the resonance of music. It is something like that, but not exactly. Because it will not be some pleasant melody, although it will be pleasant.

I am thinking of Chladni Plates, which demonstrate a pattern in sand or water when certain frequencies of vibration are applied to them.

That is one way to think about it. But that is only a representation of the structure. What we want to get at is the function. You will get to the structure by creating the function, and then the structure will be available for other functions.[40]

So what we will do is set the vibration in motion.

I have a little fear reaction. This has happened before, when I was asked to allow change. It feels like giving up control. But that is really about Trust. I know that this is something that not only needs to happen, but I also want to happen.

It does not exactly need to happen. Not right here. Because there are other opportunities. But you can be one of those opportunities if you allow it.

Just now I heard a plane overhead. That is a structure that has been built, and now the structure has a function that allows people to fly through the air, gaining travel and perspective that they would not otherwise have.

Yes, well, you can talk about it forever, or we can do it.

Haha. Of course.

---

[40] Here is an example of this structure/function relationship: A chair is an object. I can see it as a structure, as parts producing a sum (wood + nails + glue = chair). Or I can see it as a function, as a sum broken down into its parts (chair = legs + seat + back). Once the chair exists, it can have multiple uses. I can sit on it. I can use it as a shelf for stacked books. I can use it like a stool and stand on it. In a brawl, I can hold it out in front of me as a shield. I can even break up the chair and use it to make a fire. A person is also an 'object.' Once I exist, I can use my presence for multiple purposes. I can choose to feed my ego or be a conduit for spiritual energy.

Now. What I am going to ask you to do is let your body become a vortex. I see this. My body is a long vertical cone, wide above my head and narrowing into a near-point below my first chakra, below my body. There is a circular energy movement around the inside shape of the cone. There are small black beads rotating in the cone, spiraling in both directions. I can concentrate on one bead, one direction at a time. I can also allow my focus to include both directions at once. This is similar to Qigong movements that involve both sides of the body going different directions at the same time. There is the energy of each side, or each individual bead, and then there is the energy of both sides and all the beads going in multiple directions at once. *Each "bead" is one "dimension," if you will. You can incorporate as many as you like. Eventually, you will.*

I can barely manage two right now. I can sense how it will be when there are more, when there are many, like a swarm of bees, all working together harmoniously in a unity of vibration. The vibration is slower and more spacious at the top of the cone, and concentrated like a hurricane at the bottom, in the tip. Then the beads, behaving like bees, come out of the pinpoint end of the cone and disperse into the current dimension. Apparently, there can be many different colors and sizes and shapes of "bees," or beads, or dimensions. The effect is kaleidoscopic—like an acid trip, with swirling sounds and shapes and colors. This is not happening just in my head. It is a whole-being experience. Talking about it, defining it, reduces the sensation.

  The Library Man is looking at me with hidden amusement. I am trying to make this fit into something I know. I need to just allow it to Be. He turns and places his chalk on the chalk rail. He puts his hands in his pockets and shrugs. He turns his back and walks away from me. I am to practice this sensation. Just allow it. That is today's lesson.

  He turns his head and I can see him smiling. He is pleased. I love him! Love turns the beads a glowing ruby red, with silver balls orbiting each one and leaving silver streamers of stardust in their paths. It would be interesting to explore the nature of the cone and the beads under different circumstances. Experimenting with emotion, I laugh out loud and the beads turn bright blue with yellow orbiters. I mimic fear, and the whole system begins to shut down, going into slow motion with reduced-speed audio. Wow. I had been so involved in the visual that I wasn't using my ears. Life is amazing—there is so much to learn!

These are the same beads in a cone of energy that I experienced earlier, in the vision with the business woman and the braided woman. This time it had the added element of movement and color and sound. Clearly, the quality of the energy I experience is something that affects the beads and their movement, and this quality is something I can choose.

∽

To choose something positive, I have to make room for it. I have to clear out a lot of self-limiting beliefs that are constraining the energy in and around me. Many of these are internalized childhood messages like rejection, fear, hopelessness, and shame. I'd like to say that I don't believe these messages or carry those feelings. Cognitively, I know how unhelpful they are and that they don't belong to me. Past experiences have created pathways in my emotional wiring, however, and those stored feelings affect my behavior and my energy.

I decided to give back some of the messages and feelings that were obstructing my energy. I wanted to give them back to the Everything, where there is room for them without blame or other attachments, and I created a spontaneous ritual to let the messages flow out of me. I started with a marker and some birchbark. I had no idea how I was going to proceed. I let the ritual form itself as I went.

I started by using the marker to write each obstructing message, one by one, on the bark. I took my time, allowing each message to surface without judgment. I let myself experience the feelings that went with each one as I wrote it down. I cried a lot. I placed the pieces of birchbark in an empty cardboard box.

Eventually, the box was chock full of these constricting messages.

When I felt I was finished I wrapped the box in a brown paper bag, like a gift. I wrote my feelings on the outside of the box. Then I wrote my intentions for the ritual on the box. My intentions were to clear space and create opportunity, to clear space for me to manifest my purpose and to move the gifts I have been given.

I placed the box in the wood stove. There were only a few coals in there and it took quite a while for it to start burning. Not every change is a big whoosh of transformation. As I waited I was reminded of how I had invoked Kali, the goddess of fire, during cancer treatment. I had invited Kali to burn away everything I didn't need, to burn the cancer out of my body and give me a new start. I invited Kali again to help me burn these messages out of my life, to create new space and opportunity.

The box burned slowly. I sat in front of the open stove door on a stool, staying present for the entire process. I watched the wrapping smolder and char. I watched the flames lick the inside of the box and slowly consume the contents. I poked it a few times to give it more air. I prayed. When it was done only the charred ashes remained. I felt a beautiful new spaciousness inside me. In my core I was a free spirit, flowing in a long dress with bunches of flowers in my hands, legs kicking high in a dance of joy. This is what it feels like to celebrate Life! Not just existing or surviving or getting by, but taking hold of my gifts and dancing with them, moving the energy—celebrating Life!

The Library Man has his eyebrows raised. His eyes are twinkling and he has a big toothy smile under that bushy white mustache:
Ah. This is the moment we have been coming to. Positive energy. Positive energy is moving and available. You have only to choose it.
[He is waltzing around the room with his arms up and a spring in his step.]
This, we can do. There is no magic to this except the choosing of it.
[He holds up a small test tube, peering at it. There are bubbles rising from the bottom and breaking the surface of a clear liquid.]
This is what creates change—exciting the matter, the molecules, the form,

until it becomes another. You have this capacity yourself. To excite the medium which is your physical presence, to excite it with the movement of energy between one dimension and the next. The transference itself creates the energy. Vibrations. Multi-Dimensional Positive Energy, Movement.

We have been moving towards this for a long time. It is important to have cleared out some of the negative energy that was blocking the movements. Now you must be aware of, pay attention to, what you move through that cleared space. Multi-Dimensional Positive Movement. The only requirement is that it feed you.

You will feel this as Joy. That is the measuring stick. Not necessarily happiness, but Joy. Focus your activities on that which brings you Joy. Everything else will follow the way it needs to. There is no forcing. There is only riding the waves and using Joy to mark your course.

Practice this.

~ 7 ~

The Path With Joy

Spiritual practice transforms of our feelings, thoughts, and actions. It involves a willingness to make mistakes and a desire to grow and change. Spiritual practice is not a state of being, it is a path unfolding, and we are meant to travel this path with joy.

What is joy? Joy is a sensation, a feeling. Feelings are energy vibrations that happen in our body. They're difficult to describe in words because they're not physically concrete—they are experiences. Love and beauty are experiences. So are happiness and joy.

The words 'happiness' and 'joy' are sometimes used interchangeably but they are not the same. We feel happiness as pleasure, contentment, or satisfaction. Joy goes deeper—it's like happiness but with an added sense of well-being. Experiencing happiness and experiencing joy can be compared to the difference between eating chocolate cake (which is satisfying), and witnessing a beautiful sunset (where I feel like the world is amazing and I'm grateful to be in it). Eating cake is pleasure, or happiness. Admiring the sunset involves whole body well-being, which is joy.

> "Popular opinion holds that Joy is a result of being happy. I think that's backward. Joy allows you to be happy. Happy feelings are temporary. Joy is much deeper than that. True joy is untouched by circumstance."
> *-Harvey Mackay*

Life is an ongoing story of changing circumstance—sadness, loss, and trauma are part of the human condition. Our inner spiritual environment affects how we cope. It is possible to experience devastating trauma and come through the other side of it with joy. The Dalai Lama, for example, was forced into exile during a brutal political takeover. In an instant he lost his family, his community, his country, and his homeland. As a spiritual leader, he also bore the weight of this pain for all his people. He acknowledges this pain, but also chooses to reframe his trauma by viewing distress as an opportunity—an opportunity to learn more about the wider world and to exert his spiritual influence beyond his community.

Suffering is the flip side of joy. As long as we don't get stuck there, suffering can help us to appreciate life. It can bring us to joy. Cancer survivors understand this well: once you have faced the very real potential of your own death, you become grateful for the gift that is every day lived on this planet. Whether it is suffering or some other experience that opens our eyes, joy is a path that we can establish through practice.

> "Joy does not simply happen to us. We have to choose Joy and keep choosing it every day."
> -Henri Nouwen

The Netflix queen of organizing is a woman named Marie Kondo. She helps people clear out clutter in their lives by helping them sort through the physical objects in their home. She encourages them to hold each object and determine if it brings them joy. Those objects that bring them joy stay. Those that don't, go. In the end, the person is surrounded only by objects that embody joy. The process itself also reconnects the person with the sensations of joy—they repeatedly practice recognizing, feeling, and honoring it as they sort through their lives. This intentional practice of joy results in an environment that also supports it.

Another way to keep choosing joy, to purposefully make room for it, is to create retreat space. Whether this retreat lasts days, hours, or minutes, the intention is the same. I often follow the guidelines from Jennifer Louden's *The Women's Retreat Book*, which encourage us to "disengage from the externally referenced world (What should I be doing? What would others think of this?), and from the web of connections and commitments to others."[41] Retreat is not a schedule of activities. It is the creation of an energy environment that moves us out of the busyness of our everyday lives and into the freedom of creative space.

During retreat I choose to engage only in activities that feed me or free me—that bring me joy. I make two lists. One is a list of everything that is a 'No.' That includes news and social media, house cleaning and repair, paperwork piles, shopping, driving my car—everything that is a distraction from my inner life. It is possible to do any of those things mindfully, but eliminating their temptation creates an environment of inner ease. I also make a list of everything that is a 'Yes.' That includes writing, play, creativity, laughter, dancing, art, healing, hiking, meditation, mindful eating, sleep, and Doing Nothing. I travel through my time in retreat freely choosing from the Yes list in every moment. I always come out of retreat refreshed, inspired, and reconnected with the flow of the Universe.

Creating intentional space has helped me uncover hidden beliefs that are dragging down my energy. One is the idea that I can somehow 'get ahead' if I just perform more, faster, and do more things at once. I'm under the illusion that if I could achieve more in my limited time, I would somehow get through my task list and begin to experience more free time. In reality, the list is endless and doing more just makes me feel pressured and energetically dead.

'Getting Ahead' is another way to describe 'achievement.' Achievement can be big milestones, like a new job or a new home or a graduation. Achievement can also be hidden in smaller activities, like doing 'just one more thing' from my paper pile even though

---

[41] (HarperCollins, 2004), p. 3

I'm already drained. The drive to achieve can be fed by my own expectations—needing to 'contribute to society' or 'help my family/my team,' and then saying Yes to more than I can do. I often feel guilty for not doing enough.

I've learned that a lot of the things on the No list for my retreats are part of the Getting Ahead/Achievement trap, and they keep me confined in ego function. As Osho, the Zen Master says, "This moment...this herenow...is forgotten when you start thinking in terms of achieving something. When the achieving mind arises, you lose contact with the paradise you are in...Forget about sin and forget about saintliness: both are stupid...How can you live joyously?"[42]

How can I live joyously in the moment? According to Osho, it is a simple choice. "Either you can be in Existence or you can be in Self—both are not possible together. To be in the self means to be apart, to be separate...to draw a boundary line around you...The self isolates. And it makes you frozen—you are no longer flowing...In Love the boundaries disappear; in joy also the boundaries disappear."[43]

During my time in retreat I allow confining boundaries to disappear. I do not want the benefits of retreat to end when I re-enter my daily life. Part of the reason to go on retreat is to reconnect with the sensations and behaviors that I wish to manifest outside of retreat. In order to continue the fruits of retreat after I emerge, I use this mantra: Open Up To the Joy of Existing.

༄

Sometimes our best intentions fall short. We have all been conditioned by our past experiences, and that conditioning can get in the way. Our autonomic system is constantly scanning the environment for cues that we may be in danger and activates our fight, flight or freeze reactions. This system isn't great at telling time.

---

[42] *Osho Zen Tarot* (St. Martin's Press, 1994), p. 132

[43] Ibid, p. 122.

It can't tell the difference between a current experience and the memory of a past traumatic event. Sometimes, our body reacts to something from the past as if it is happening right now. This is often a reaction to a sensory association with the past trauma—a sound, taste, smell, or emotional vibration. Things in the present that cause a reaction to past events are called *triggers*. Triggers re-create the body's stress response, inducing fear and a flood of stress hormones such as adrenaline.

Triggering has become a mainstream concept. There are trigger warnings in books, before movies, and during news programs. Viewers are given the chance to limit or avoid their exposure to triggering content in order to limit a triggered stress response. The word 'trigger' has entered our everyday vocabulary.

There is a mirror concept which is not yet mainstream. It was introduced by licensed clinical social worker Deb Dana,[44] and is called a *glimmer*. Glimmers are also reactions produced by the autonomic nervous system, but they are positive cues that bring us back to a sense of joy, safety, and connection. They have a calming effect on our nervous system.

Just as triggers can be avoided, glimmers can be pursued. You can develop your own glimmers. Some of them might include: feeling the warmth of the sun or a fresh cool breeze on your skin, smelling lavender or bread baking, seeing a sun-sparkled lake or a starry sky, petting a dog or a cat, listening to leaves rustle in the trees or waves lapping on a shore, tasting a nice cup of tea or coffee, smiling at a stranger, or smiling for no reason. Glimmers produce a sense of ease and calm. Any amount is beneficial and worthwhile. Sometimes just thinking about them can be helpful.

Recognizing small, positive moments over and over can begin to reshape our mental and physical health. Once we begin to see and acknowledge glimmers, we can begin to look for and experience more of them. We can even set a "glimmer intention"

---

[44] See Deb Dana's book *The Polyvagal Theory in Therapy: Engaging the Rhythm of Regulation* (Norton, 2018).

such as: I'm going to look for one glimmer this morning. You can keep a glimmer journal to look back on. You can ask a friend to go on a glimmer journey with you!

Even though I regularly practice moving energy in a positive way, I am still sometimes challenged to do so. On difficult days, when I'm not able to relax or center, I'm unable to see the spiritual opportunities before me. It helps to notice when I am in this darkness, stuck, focusing on Points.

The Library Man: *You have been busy moving your energy from Point to Point, focusing on getting to the next point and the next. So you know how draining this activity is. It is not a good way to be using the gift of your physical presence. It dissipates your energy stores rather than renewing them. That is why you are so tired.*

Really, it is the opposite of what you are being asked to do. You have to be able to allow your energy to exist in Space. That is a way of freeing up the Points. Rather than try to limit their movement, you want to be allowing for change.

There is this idea that a Point is a static object, something that is fixed. Really, it is just a set of coordinates in a specific location. When you allow your energy to exist in Space, it frees up the Points to take in and move energy. This action changes the energy, but also changes the Points themselves.

This is what the Universe wants to do—flow. It does not want to stop and stagnate. In fact, it is not able to stop. It will continue to flow, but its flow will be restrained and restricted. It will not flow evenly or well. It will have to go around places that are blocked. This creates different energy pathways that are not as smooth or helpful.

I am thinking of an example like the human heart, which is designed to be strong and smooth and constantly pumping and flowing. When there are blockages to this flow it creates back-ups in the channels that carry the blood, and limits where the blood can go. There is less oxygen and nourishment for both the heart itself and for other organs and tissues. There can be damage to the heart and vessels and, eventually, there is the possibility of fatal errors.

This is a fair example. It is important, for both the heart itself and for the entire body, that the heart function smoothly. All Points, everywhere, whether they are planets or atoms, function in this way. The energy has to move. That is what Life Force is. It is Movement.

To use your own example of energy habits, you can see how lack of flow is impeding your overall health. Focusing on tasks and deadlines and other externally generated goals means you are focusing on Points. You feel that if you just get these things done, you will be able to sit back and relax. But through these actions you have created an energy practice which is focused on shutting down, rather than freeing up, your flow.

It is not possible to completely eliminate the need to accomplish some of these things. But you must address the way in which you do them. Quality is important. Not the quality of your effort, but the quality of your actions. The desired quality is openness and flow. In order to embody this quality, you must have your energy aligned with Space, with all of the space around and within everything. The Everything. Then you can be aware of the Points as they present themselves, you can touch them briefly, and you can move on. You will be focused on movement.

It's not that you don't care, that you don't use your heart. Moving energy with your heart, and with your intellect, and your mind, are all important parts of being in physical form. But it is the movement *of energy that is important. Not the nailing down, the deciding for sure, the labeling and defining. The Movement. Both happiness and pain are forms of attachment. Holding on to either of these means you are forming a Point and restricting energy. True Joy will appear when energy is given the freedom of Space and Flow.*

Giving energy the freedom of Space and Flow is a state that I actively create. While it is not passive, it is also not intended to be something that I push for—it's not work. It's more like curating energy opportunities. There are choices to be made. The choice to allow movement has to be made over and over. I am choosing Space and Flow when I say *and embody*: I thank the Universe and The Teachers for bringing me to this point in Time; I have been guided to this place where I am, in a stream of energy connected to The Zone, connected with more dimensions.

This helps me see my purpose in context. When I begin to wonder about how my intention is manifesting, the flow begins to stagnate. I've focused a lot of energy on getting my books into print, for example. There have been many obstacles, notably a side journey into cancer treatment and then the shut-downs of the Covid pandemic. I'm challenged to see the point in putting all this energy into the books. When I focus on that, on feeling stalled out, I come to a dead end in the flow. When I go back to talking about being guided to the place where I currently am, in a stream of energy to connected to more dimensions, I feel myself open up again. I feel called to the information in these books. Then my whole body is buzzing with aliveness, the energy flow is back.

Universal Wisdom: *We want you to practice your energy states. We want you to be in Multi-Dimensional Positive Energy, no matter what you are doing. There is energy coming in at this time and that is your access point. Many people are struggling right now, with reactive energy. I too am distressed at the social injustice happening right now, happening as I am typing this.*[45]

You are not there. That is not your current environment. You are removed, precisely because that keeps you on the path of energy awareness and movement. Remember movement. Movement in the Sea of Energy. Multi-Dimensional Positive Energy, MDPE, is your shorthand for communication with The Zone.

It helps me to keep repeating these words: I have been guided to the place where I am—in a stream of energy connected to The Zone, connected to more dimensions. A stream of energy connected to The Zone, to more dimensions.

As soon as I stop, I am once again distracted by culture and society, feeling the need to jump up and *do* something that makes a change. Yet I am small and powerless…and that just takes me away

---

[45] Refers to the law enforcement murder of George Floyd, and the resulting protests and riots in Minneapolis, Minnesota.

from the expansive feeling, from transcendence. I need to return to faith, to my faith in a process that is larger than me, certainly larger than Me The Ego. That is a good reminder about ego and spirit and soul. The Spirit-fed life leads me on my Soul Path.
You have entered another phase of your Earth-Spirit classroom. It is good to sense this, but not to push there. Let it happen, like everything so far.
Create a space of freedom and ease, and then see what comes into it. *This is creative energy. This is creativity in motion. Be the energy you wish to manifest. It will all be known in time.*

༄

Developing a new energy configuration is not a project, it's a path. A path is a collection of energy experiences created by the flow of being. Our old paths will not serve us in the multi-dimensional re-arrangements of The Shift. We will have to create new ones.
The Library Man: *I want to talk about moving energy in the next dimension. This is something you are going to need, and can no longer wait until the moment is ripe. It has arrived. Life is going to change in ways you cannot imagine.*
I have to check myself here. I have been trying to tamp down my growing panic. The climate is going wacko, world governments and world economies are going wacko. It all feels like a house of cards. Things are out of balance. I am most concerned for the children, for all children. I can die today and I will have had a good life, but the younger people must struggle on with what is.
[He is chuckling to himself].
Do you really think that this is the first time of imbalance? It has happened all throughout history. It is good to be aware. It is detrimental to become over-involved in things you have no control over. You must bring your focus to a level that is within your scope of practice.

Your scope of practice involves personal contact. It is no coincidence that you were introduced to Samite—he is embodying the kind of work that you are also made for.[46] *Personal contact. Direct transmission of the vibration. It can happen in many ways.*

Your purpose is to be a clear channel, to let the Teachings come through you and move to others, to be a mouthpiece. There will be a chance to become this mouthpiece and you must take it. Of course, you will be afraid, because it will not be easy to recognize where that path is going to take you. You will recognize it by the resonance, by the energy it emanates and the energy it energizes in you. I cannot tell you what this offering is, but I can tell you how to prepare for it.

To be ready to take this path, you must be ready to move yourself into Timelessness. It is not just a thought, or a way of thinking. It is a way of organizing your being.

I am having trouble staying on track. I keep bringing myself back to breath and centering and expanding. I feel a pulse of energy moving horizontally at my heart level.

This is where it starts, at the heart level. This is why we have spoken so much about compassion, because that is one of the first steps. There is awareness, then transcendence, then compassion, and then movement of compassion. It is the movement of compassion, not just sitting and experiencing it, but moving that energy. And not just from you, but through you. The energy has to come from the Universe, and come through you as a physical vibration on its way to entering another energy field.

I sense that this is about connecting dimensions—that when I bring Universal energy through my body in the form of compassion, and move it to another person, I am also moving it back into the Universe through them. It is a connecting of dimensions using physical form as a medium.

Something like that.

If Space is continuous, the energy must change in some way by going through the physical medium?

Space is continuous. Through Space, energy is moving in and out of

---

[46]Samite Mulondo is an African musician who uses storytelling and music to effect vibrational change.

Points. You and others are Points. Moving the energy between Points energizes the space it moves through. It is good to understand this, but it is most important to do it, to experience it. This compassionate connection is vital energy. It is Life Force. This is your purpose, to move Life Force.

What Samite is describing is this process, of bringing the gift to others, of transferring the gift through himself.
I see how he uses his music, which is a universal energy. The storytelling helped connect the music. I could relate to his travels and his connections with people, that is a lot like the richness I experienced when I worked as a community nurse. I am challenged to see how this transfers to work as an author, where the medium is written words? Oh. But it is not the words so much as the resulting vibration. And speaking the words is a greater transmission than just reading them silently. So you are saying that there will be some kind of speaking involved.

I was very shy for much of my life. It did not feel safe to speak out. I have overcome this fear, for the most part, first by practicing as a nurse and then by putting myself out there selling these books face-to-face.
You will not need bravery so much as leaning forward. You will want to connect to all that is coming. You are ready. You are to move energy between Points, and those Points are humans. It is to be a direct transmission, which necessarily implies close contact, in person. It is not sitting at home and fretting, it is moving and enjoyment, it is embodying the teachings. You are made for this. No worries. Eyes open. Energy clear. Clean connections. Be yourself, all of yourself.

<u>Sometimes I Forget</u>
I sometimes forget
that I was created for Joy.

My mind is too busy.
My Heart is too heavy

for me to remember
that I have been
called to dance
the Sacred dance of life.

I was created to smile
To Love
To be lifted up
And to lift others up.

O' Sacred One
Untangle my feet
from all that ensnares.
Free my soul.
That we might
Dance
and that our dancing
might be contagious.
~*Hafiz* [47]

We are here, on this planet, with billions of people. Every one of us is a spirit walking, dancing the sacred dance of life. Sharing this gift with others is a *feeling*. It is the vibration of being simultaneously present to both the infinite outer world and the infinite inner world. It is consciously choosing to embody the vibration of Joy.

The place where we are standing right now, in the present, is located on the foundation built by all our relations. We have been given this platform, this gift, as a place to continue building. We are building the future by the choices we make now. We are standing in the matrix, in the blueprint of all that has come before. We have the freedom and the power, the responsibility, to build a future. This is

---

[47] Hafiz is a well-known Persian poet of the 12th century.

the doorway we are stepping through with The Shift. We are making the future. We are stepping into The Next World.

We are standing within the matrix, where we exist on many planes. Once we loosen out attachment to the five-sense world, we are able to access those planes. There, we receive the information we need to continue on our path. I once woke from an interesting dream which I could not remember at all, but I was clearly aware of receiving instruction. I woke from this teaching hearing the words "I am the essence of Time."

The Women's Collective: *As you noted, you were receiving instruction in your dream state. This is happening all the time, since this is one of the purposes of Spirit—to be connected and informing multiple dimensions simultaneously. It is not always possible to bring that learning directly into the physical world, as the language and constructs to support it are not readily available. It seems that you would like to try, so it may be worthwhile to continue here.*

First, we have to tell you that not everything you learn is applicable to the physical dimension. It may help you travel the arc of your Soul Path, but in another energy manifestation. So do not be too concerned if it does not seem to fit. It fits somewhere. But possibly not where you can see it. At any rate, you may be able to feel it, especially if you are connected elsewhere. So let us try.

We will start by saying that nothing exists in Time. It only exists in the essence of Time. Time does in fact exist, but it is a mutable element. You know this well—ten minutes sometimes seems like an hour and in another situation an hour seems like ten minutes.

Time is fluid. It is just a reference point, like location. They are constantly moving and changing. Five-sense reality attempts to nail down time and space, to make them stable. This is what creates the physical reality where you exist.

Then physical reality really is just a dream, an illusion.

It is, and it isn't. Without the stability of the physical world, your body would not exist and you would not be able to do the important work, have the energy impact in the Universe, that is being asked of you.

This is related to the contract that you come into this world with. You come in with specific energy tasks, to manifest and move energy in a way that benefits the Everything. It is a struggle, because being in physical form has its own challenges and distractions. But it is all part of the process. The journey. The journey of your spirit walking the Earth.

[My own thoughts are intruding here, and I am struggling to stay out of it.]

This is why it is difficult to do the teaching in waking dream, because then you are busy walking the Earth, and trying to fit this into that structure. It is bigger than that. Much bigger. So big that you cannot even imagine it. But you can *feel it.*

Do you want to continue.

Yes. I will try to let go of my expectations.

Good. Allowing is the space where this can happen.

As we were saying, you come onto this plane with a group of energy directives. These directives have at their core the movement of energy. Everything in the Universe is connected energetically. When you, in physical form, move energy, then you are affecting the vibration of everything that you are connected to.

I can see the Connecting Point, related to the connecting place that Carlos Castaneda described, just behind my upper back. It has innumerable strings of energy traveling through it. When I stretch, the entire web attached to me stretches also.

This is why it is so important to choose wisely when you take action. Action of any kind. These threads, connecting you and Everything, are conduits of information. Not unlike fiber optic cables, except that what is being transferred is millions of times more powerful and multi-faceted. The energy of this information is coming from vast numbers of other planes, including all of the connections made by your ancestors during their lives, and all of their ancestors, and on and on.

This is where we add the element of Time, of mutable time, because all of these "times" do exist simultaneously, in you. You are the movement of energy created by the journeys of your ancestors. Not just your immediate blood relatives, of course, but all of the incarnations of all of the humans and all of the sentient beings and even more than that. This is the expanse of influence that is more than you will ever be able to comprehend. Suffice to say it is infinite.

So here is this incredible treasure of information, available to you always. When you expand your awareness, your consciousness, it is possible to tap into any of it. Of course, it includes all of the "time" that has ever existed and will ever exist. This is beyond even infinity. You can come and go in these frames of reference. As long as you have a physical body, you will be somewhat limited in where you can travel. That is why it is so important to be in the dream state of sleeping—it allows you to travel and refresh with less of the physical dimension weighing you down.

The Essence of Time is what is carrying the information in the threads. The Essence of Time is created through movement. It is motion that brings anything to another location, whether that location is Time, Space, or anything else. (Yes, there is something else.)

This is directly related to the discussion of Point and Zone. "Things" in motion are the Points. The space between them is Zone. As you know, everything is made up of Points, every Point is both part of and made up of other Points. They are all joined by the space between them and this Zone is continuous. Everything is made of this Point-Zone relationship. And it is not the Point or the Zone that creates energy, but the relationship between them. The threads are streams of this relationship energy.

Of course you cannot possibly comprehend this using the primitive constructs of science. You can only comprehend this intuitively, using the energy senses of your body.

I wonder, who in my dream was saying *I* am the Essence of Time? *Everything. Everything is energized by the essence of Time, by the energy of the relationship between Point and Zone. It is a vibration. A movement. It could be you. It could be us. It could be. It could just Be.*

༄

I am a spirit walking the Earth. It is important to remember to not take in too much ego-drama, or world-drama, to let it slide by or move through me. My true purpose is to embody spiritual energy on the physical plane. To connect with the vibrations of peace, beauty, and joy. Focus. Be mindful of where I rest my attention.

After practicing meditation for quite some time, I finally realized that I am not just sitting there waiting for my mind to quiet or for something to show up. I'm practicing transcendence, the movement of energy into the arrangement of expanded consciousness. I am practicing feeling and *being* in transcendence. That message is so clear and so simple, and it just keeps repeating over and over no matter what the circumstance: practice transcendence, exist in the larger context. Expand.

The Women's Collective: *This is the message we have been trying to convey. Sometimes we work through specific problems, like relationship issues, and sometimes we are looking at bigger problems, like coping with world issues. But it really all comes down to the same message— that it is time to expand the energy footprint of humans.*

It's ironic that humans are talking about reducing their energy footprint, but are talking about how many geologic resources are getting burned up to support our physical plane lifestyle.

These things go together. By reducing their 'carbon footprint,' people will need to stop focusing on things, on physical plane objects, on Points.

Reducing focus on things helps expand the focus on relationships. Relationship is the energy that connects one thing with another, a joining through the movement of energy between one thing and the next, between multiple things simultaneously. People have been trained to focus on things as the source of energy movement. The fleeting vibration of pleasure is but a hint of the greater vibration of joy. Joy is the vibration that lasts long after the initial contact is made. It lasts because it is a different wavelength, one which contains echos, in the present, of the past and the future. It can be recalled and felt again. It can be manifested without any contact with a physical object. It can exist on its own and be magnified through intention. It can reach others through the time-space continuum. Joy is one of the vibrations of expansion, of larger context, of multi-dimensional effect.

You can start by asking, "what is good about this?" whenever you take on a project or activity. Look at what is good, not as a distraction from that which is not-good, but as a place of reference for increasing your positive vibration. Yes, positive vibration is a choice. It is not pollyanna denial or painting over decay. It is a choice to manifest the greater good in all actions and thoughts. It is connection with Universal Life Force, with multi-dimensional positive energy. It is a conscious choice to allow this connection and then to magnify it through the energy of your physical presence. It is the use of the gift of your physical body for the improvement of the Universe. It is recognizing the bigger picture, the infinite picture, and your ability and responsibility to be mindful of what you add to it. It's not just something you talk about. It's not just something you do. It's something you participate in, with your full heart and mind and body.

These are the actual teachings of the spirit-person named Jesus. To embody the Love of the Universe and assist others in their journey to also embody this Love. Any other social or political or financial process does not meet this goal. Lead by example, not by coercion. Open your heart and mind to this message, no matter what form it takes, even in religious context. You have been shutting out great opportunities because you dislike this coercion. Do not place your attention there. Place your attention on the Love of the Universe, on Life Force, and embody joy.

It is written in the [akashic] records, "and so you shall let your fears and your judgment fall away, and become a messenger of these messages." You must be present in the echo when you speak, for then the echo will come through you, and others will hear it, and you will assist them in this transformation called evolution, in to the next thing, the Next World, which awaits you.

Go now. Place yourself in the echo. Make your life one with it.